"*The Polyvagal Solution* guides readers in r heritage as a coregulated, connected species. vagal theory, this practical book reveals how the vagus nerve influences stress and serenity. With profound insights and exercises, readers will learn to neutralize stress responses, fostering balance and resilience. This accessible guide empowers individuals to harness the vagus nerve's power for a more connected, balanced, and fulfilling life."

—**Stephen W. Porges, PhD**, distinguished university scientist at Indiana University, and creator of polyvagal theory

"Rebecca Kase masterfully bridges the science of stress and the art of self-discovery in this must-read. With clear explanations and transformative exercises, she empowers readers to understand their unique nervous systems and create a personalized path to resilience. This book is an essential guide for stress relief and burnout prevention—practical, insightful, and ready to use from page one."

—**Cait Donovan**, keynote speaker; burnout expert; host of *FRIED. The Burnout Podcast*; and author of *The Bouncebackability Factor*

"Making knowledge from the psychological professions more available and accessible to ordinary folks is an imperative in modern times. Rebecca Kase rises to this challenge beautifully in *The Polyvagal Solution*. Even those of us who find neuroscience difficult to comprehend can get something out of this book and be more empowered in our healing as a result. Practical, clinically sound, and useful, *The Polyvagal Solution* is an excellent resource for the general public and clinical professions alike, and I will look forward to recommending it."

—**Jamie Marich, PhD, LPCC-S, REAT, RYT-500**, founder of The Institute for Creative Mindfulness, and author of *Dissociation Made Simple*, *Trauma and the 12 Steps*, and many other books in the field of trauma recovery

The
POLYVAGAL
SOLUTION

Vagus Nerve-Calming Practices to
Soothe Stress, Ease Emotional Overwhelm,
and Build Resilience

REBECCA KASE, LCSW

New Harbinger Publications, Inc.

Publisher's Note

This publication is designed to provide accurate and authoritative information in regard to the subject matter covered. It is sold with the understanding that the publisher is not engaged in rendering psychological, financial, legal, or other professional services. If expert assistance or counseling is needed, the services of a competent professional should be sought.

NEW HARBINGER PUBLICATIONS is a registered trademark of New Harbinger Publications, Inc.

New Harbinger Publications is an employee-owned company.

Copyright © 2025 by Rebecca Kase
New Harbinger Publications, Inc.
5720 Shattuck Avenue
Oakland, CA 94609
www.newharbinger.com

All Rights Reserved

Cover design by Amy Daniel

Acquired by Wendy Millstine and Ryan Buresh

Edited by Kandace Little

Library of Congress Cataloging-in-Publication Data on file

Printed in the United States of America

27   26   25

10   9   8   7   6   5   4   3   2   1   First Printing

This book is dedicated to Stephen W. Porges for his years of research and embodied presence as a thought leader.

Dr. Porges, your work has made the world a better place.

Contents

Foreword

It is commonly recognized that stress has a significant impact on our bodies, minds, emotions, and behaviors. You can likely recall times when your mind raced as your heartbeat and breath quickened. Perhaps, in response to stress you felt panicky. Maybe you even resorted to knee-jerk reactions in your relationships that were not fully thought through. Indeed, these responses to stress are universal. Moreover, when stress is chronic the consequences are more significant. Physically, we see increased risks for high blood pressure and heart disease, inflammation and chronic pain, headaches, diabetes, and menstrual problems in women. Mentally, there is a greater risk for anxiety, depression, cognitive decline, and sleep problems. Having tools to help you manage stress is essential for your health.

The body's stress response system has been studied for over a century by scientists such as William James, Walter Cannon, and Hans Seyle, who began to illuminate the underpinnings of your autonomic nervous system. Simply put, your autonomic nervous system comprises two pathways. The sympathetic nervous system is your metaphorical gas pedal that has long been associated with the fight-or-flight response. In contrast, the parasympathetic nervous system provides the metaphorical brakes that allow you to slow down, rest, and digest. Using this basic understanding of the nervous system, the field of psychology has sought out ways to offset the harm of chronic exposure to stress.

Since stress is typically an expression of an overactive sympathetic system, it was initially thought that the best way to buffer stress was to help us access our relaxation response. Unfortunately, this approach to stress management was only partially successful. This is because the parasympathetic system does not always lead to restoration of the body and mind. Rather, in times of extreme danger, the parasympathetic system can also initiate a feigned death response by rapidly slowing down your heart rate and respiration. How could the parasympathetic system have both of these reactions? Dr. Stephen W. Porges developed the polyvagal theory to better understand these paradoxical expressions of the parasympathetic system. His work illuminated a more complex picture of the nervous system and guided us to a more nuanced approach to stress management.

One of the essential elements of polyvagal theory is the recognition that we need to befriend our sympathetic nervous system. This allows us to reclaim our life force energy in service of what allows us to feel playful, joyful, and excited. Furthermore, a new definition of health of our autonomic nervous systems is the ability to transition smoothly and easefully between the sympathetic and parasympathetic branches. Doing so builds the tone of our vagus nerve, which serves as a biological marker of resilience.

Since knowledge is a foundation of change, having a working understanding of your stress response system provides the keys to help free you from automatic reactions to stressful life events. Rebecca Kase has given you a map of your brain and body. Within the pages of this book, she guides you to implement a wide range of tools that help you create greater balance in your life. She explains how your nervous system is wired for connection and encourages you to lean into your superpower of coregulation. She then mindfully guides you home to yourself through body-based exercises and practices rooted in loving-kindness. Rebecca reminds us that this "home is where the heart is" and that you have within you a biological blueprint that can enhance your overall health.

—Arielle Schwartz, PhD

Chapter 1

Meet Your Vagus Nerve

Stress is the ultimate party crasher. Like death and taxes, it's always lurking, ready to ruin a good time. It's one thing we all share and can all count on. No matter how much money you have, where you live, what the status of your family drama is, whether you like dogs or cats… stress is guaranteed. While many social, political, physical, emotional, and economic factors contribute to your risk of stress, every living creature gets its share of stress many times, in many ways, over the course of a lifetime. But while it may be inevitable, we don't have to resign ourselves to a lifetime of being a pent-up ball of stress. Yes, it's possible to reclaim your chill.

Stress comes in many forms, sizes, and doses. Bills, traffic, work deadlines, a full inbox, political and societal unrest, climate change, and having too much on the to-do list is stressful for everyone. Then, there are sneaky stressors—those things that emotionally overwhelm us that no one ever expects to tackle, such as health scares, breakups, and job loss. These are considerable stressors that can turn us upside down and leave us feeling messy inside. Some of us have also experienced traumatic stress, such as combat, sexual assault, racism, bullying, or gun violence. So yes, stress comes in many shapes and sizes and, therefore, has varying degrees of impact.

Because stress and emotional overwhelm are inevitable, your body comes preprogrammed with ways of responding. Thanks to millions of years of evolution, your DNA has helped to program your mind and body with stress responses. The tight jaw, sleepless nights, and panic are all ways your body is wired to respond to stress. Even though those annoying symptoms can make life challenging, they are actually indicators that your body is doing its job—trying to help you overcome the challenge. This may sound absurd, but after reading this book, you will better understand your stress patterns and see your body as your best friend for dealing with dysregulation and overwhelm.

Common symptoms of stress include anxiety, depression, sleep problems, changes to appetite, digestive issues, depression, a weakened immune system, and many more. This leaves you susceptible to illness, impulsivity, interpersonal challenges, cravings for legal or illegal substances, chronic pain, and other forms of dis-ease and discomfort. You are probably aware of a plethora of ways you respond to stress. But have you ever paused to consider what is driving those symptoms, why you respond to stress the way you do, or how you can work with your neurobiology in those moments of meltdown?

Your nervous system is front and center when it comes to feeling stressed out and overwhelmed. When you're stressed, your nervous system is kicked into gear, activating responses that produce those pesky emotional and physical symptoms. Your nervous system is the driving force to feeling stressed and overwhelmed or regulated and balanced. A chronically stressed, dysregulated, malnourished nervous system can make life feel like a constant uphill battle and leave you feeling wrecked. Similarly, a balanced, resilient, well-cared-for nervous system is the key to happiness, peace, joy, and emotional regulation. Your nervous system can be your greatest asset and resource in this thing called life.

Stress doesn't have to get the best of you. Numerous self-help books offer clever strategies for dealing with stress. There's a wealth of useful information out there on highly effective techniques such as yoga, meditation, mindfulness, and therapeutic self-help skills. However, much of the self-help literature is missing a crucial factor: understanding your nervous system. Learning how your nervous system works clues you into its secrets so you can harness its natural, adaptive powers to live a more balanced and happy life. A life full of meaningful relationships, rest, play, and health. Your nervous system holds the keys to all of this. Learning how your nervous system works allows you to work with it.

And when you can work with your nervous system, stress no longer feels like an out-of-control experience. Which is exactly the focus of this book.

The Vagus Nerve and Emotional Wellness

Your nervous system is a vast, expansive system that communicates via electrical signals and neurotransmitters that pass through cells or neurons. It is an information superhighway, sending information between your brain and your organs, cells, and tissues. It plays a role in digestion, immunity, physical movements, sleep cycles, relationships, behaviors, and emotions. When you feel regulated, your nervous system is regulated. When you feel dysregulated, specific neural pathways are the root cause.

There are trillions of nerve cells in your body and a multitude of processes and hormones that contribute to the uncomfortable things that you associate with stress. Let's be clear that when it comes to stress and feeling emotionally overwhelmed, there is no single cell, nerve, or thing that happens that is the one and only culprit. However, there is a specific nerve that has a considerable impact on how stressed you feel at any given moment. Learning about this nerve and how to work with it can give you access to strategies and insights to better cope. That nerve is called the *vagus nerve*.

The vagus nerve has a significant influence on your emotional state. When your brain perceives a stressor, it cues this nerve to activate a series of reactions to protect and defend you. When the vagus nerve gives the command, virtually every bodily system responds in specific, evolutionarily rehearsed ways. Because this nerve is so powerful, learning to befriend it and care for it can give you the knowledge and strategies you need to live a more balanced life.

Unlocking the power of your vagus nerve is available to you with the wisdom of polyvagal theory. You might consider polyvagal theory an instruction manual outlining how the vagus works, why it does what it does, and what it needs to promote health and wellness for your mind, body, and soul. Developed by Stephen Porges, this scientific theory offers a treasure trove of information to help you bounce back from stress, be more resilient, and live a more peaceful life. Even if brain science isn't your cup of tea, don't roll your eyes or toss this book out just yet! This is your guide for translating the complex science of polyvagal theory into easy-to-understand explanations and strategies. You'll learn how to integrate polyvagal theory into your daily life through concrete skills and techniques you can use anywhere. With practice, you can learn to use the power of your vagus nerve to your benefit.

As a licensed psychotherapist, trauma survivor, and owner of a large training business, I understand, personally and professionally, the toll that stress can take on a person. Learning polyvagal theory and harnessing its wisdom has been a life-changing experience for me and my clients. I use these techniques every day in my personal life, and I have found the more I use them, the less I need them. As my nervous system becomes more resilient, I feel overwhelmed and stressed less often, but when I do, I can bounce back pretty quickly. I feel more confident in myself because fewer things can knock me down. I trust life more because I trust that I can handle whatever comes my way. My clients who learn these skills report similar outcomes. More balance and happiness, less emotional overwhelm. Many clients have shared that they turn to these techniques daily to manage symptoms of anxiety, depression, PTSD, and addiction. Learning to tap into the power of your vagus can be a game changer in the battle with stress.

Connect with Your Vagus Nerve

Vagus stands for "wanderer" or "vagabond." It is the second longest nerve in your body, coming in as runner-up to the sciatic nerve. This nerve "wanders" the body and has a lot of destinations it connects to— the wanderlust nerve.

The vagus is not one nerve but a bundle of nerves, efferent and afferent, that carry information between the brain and body. *Efferent* nerves carry information from the brain to the body. In contrast, *afferent* nerves carry information from the body to the brain. The vagus is the brain-body connection, as it sends information in both directions.

The vagus nerve communicates with muscles of the inner ear, the muscles around the eyes, the muscles in the face, the throat, the vocal cords, the lungs, the heart, and all of the abdominal organs. When this nerve is activated by stress, it can cause changes throughout these locations. Because the vagus nerve connects to so many muscles and organs, stress is a full-body experience.

Here are some conditions associated with vagal dysfunction:

- Depression

- Anxiety

- PTSD

- Addiction

- Disordered eating

- Difficulties with attention, learning, and concentration

- Difficulties in interpersonal relationships

- Digestive issues

- Dizziness or fainting

- Heart and blood pressure issues

- Breathing difficulties

- Muscle tension and pain

- Teeth grinding

- Ringing in ears

- Sweating

And that's not an exhaustive list! But it's probably enough of a list for you to identify that the vagus nerve has a whole lot of power and influence.

When this nerve is in good health, your mind and body are more likely to be regulated and balanced. Digestion, immunity, and respiration function as they were designed to. You feel happy, peaceful, and fulfilled. Your relationships are more likely to be in good standing. And you're more likely to get restful, restorative sleep. When this nerve is activated out of fear and stress, it disrupts this normal homeostasis. As a result, your body can't function optimally, and lots of things can go awry. We suffer emotionally, physically, and relationally if this nerve is constantly activated out of stress, threat, or danger.

To begin, let's take a moment for you to make a formal introduction with your small but mighty vagus nerve.

Connect with Your Vagus Nerve Exercise

Find a comfortable and quiet place where you can turn inward and reflect.

We will move through points in the body that the vagus connects with. As you read, bring your attention to that place in your body. You might bring your hands or fingers to rest on the area described. Move through this slowly, pausing at each location for ten to thirty seconds:

Middle ear muscles

Muscles around the eyes

Muscles around the cheek and jaw

The vocal cords

The esophagus

The lungs

The heart

The digestive organs

Slowly tune into each point, and remain curious about any sensation you experience. Do you notice tension, softness, constriction, or energy moving in these spaces? Or you may notice nothing. Observe your experience and be curious while remaining free of judgment.

What happens to those vagal connection points when you're stressed or emotionally dysregulated? Move through each point again, and consider how those spaces feel in these three different emotional states:

"What happens at those points of vagal connection when I feel..."

sad, depressed, down in the dumps

anxious, worried, or angry

peaceful, happy, and balanced

Make a note of the different sensations and physical states you experience in these bodily areas when in each of those emotional states. You'll probably notice that there are some considerable differences!

Now that you've met your vagus, expand your awareness. Next time you feel frustrated, annoyed, angry, shut down, or really good, notice how these spaces in your body are responding. Doing so is the first step to befriending your vagus nerve and becoming aware of your stress responses.

Pressure Points

Emotional overwhelm and stress go hand in hand. Something in our life "stresses" our mind and body, leading our nervous system to produce physiological and psychological reactions that we call "stress," "overwhelm," "anxiety," "depression," and so forth. Stress is the common thread that runs through all of us, yet what stresses us out can vary significantly from one person to another. Rush hour traffic might seem like a breeze for one person and a nightmare for another; bills and work may be grueling for some, while others experience extreme stress from political news or interactions with their family—we all have unique pressure points. As you begin this journey of befriending your vagus nerve, building awareness of your unique pressure points is a good place to start. That is, learning to identify your unique triggers or stressors is key. I call these *pressure points*.

Pressure points are things, people, places, or experiences that cause your nervous system and vagus to activate a defensive stress response. They are your individual "hot" buttons that, when pushed, can lead to inner turmoil. We each have unique "pressure points" that can push us outside our comfort zone and flare symptoms of stress. Our pressure points can stem from the unique way we are individually wired, the unresolved trauma we carry, our cultural experiences, our individual life history, and our present circumstances. For example, you might find that you cannot tolerate loud noises because they instantly cause you to feel overwhelmed and anxious. There's no rhyme or reason. It's just how you're wired. That would be a pressure point based on your unique biology. There might be a specific person who is a pressure point because they have hurt you and caused you pain. This would be a pressure point connected to your personal history. A circumstantial pressure point would be feeling stressed because of a pressing work deadline.

As you can see, pressure points can vary greatly. Some are because of your unique biology, others due to your history, and some due to your current state of affairs. Some pressure points remain consistent, while others change. Pressure points are unique to you and can ebb and flow over time.

Learning to recognize your pressure points gives you the opportunity to be proactive and preventative in managing your emotional state and stress responses. Learning to catch your nervous system getting activated is a great way to prevent things from turning into a five-alarm fire.

Identify Your Pressure Points

Following is a list of common pressure points. Write down all the pressure points that cause you considerable distress. Add any additional pressure points you identify that aren't listed here.

Work or school	Children	Friends
Extended family and friends	Partner/spouse/ intimate relationships	Drugs/alcohol/ addictive substances
Finances	Physical health	Mental health
Home life	Chores	Animals or pets
Housing	Food	Basic needs
Distressing memories from the past	Politics	Racism or prejudice
Climate	Caregiving	Day-to-day chores
Travel	Life transitions	Death or loss
Sensory stressors (e.g., sounds, overhead lights, smells, textures)	Specific places (e.g., the grocery store, the airport)	Specific events (e.g., the Fourth of July, the school fair, family BBQs)

Identify how often you experience these pressure points. Daily, weekly, monthly, 24/7?

Can you identify which points are:

1. Just how you're wired?

2. Due to your unique history and experiences?

3. Circumstantial?

If you're uncertain about a few, that's okay. You don't have to know it all.

Take time now to journal and reflect. What stands out to you? What new insights can you gain? Are there themes? How can you use this information to be more proactive and preventative?

The Art of Listening

When you come down with something like the flu, COVID, or a cold, your body gives you a heads-up. It gets your attention and informs you that you might be sick with symptoms. Noticing the scratchy throat, watery eyes, or muscle aches allows you to do something about it. Awareness of symptoms is the first step to intervention. While no intervention will necessarily stop the flu or a cold in its tracks, there are things you can do to help your immune system better the odds. You might get extra sleep, drink more fluids, call your doctor, or take medication or supplements to bounce back. If your body didn't give you those signs and signals, you'd have little to no opportunity to intervene and help it out. Therefore, symptoms are, in part, the body's means of communicating information to you so you can take action. This is not to say every illness or disease comes with clear warning signs. But at some point, you become aware of the symptoms. The more attuned you are to listening to your body, the quicker you can catch the symptoms and the quicker you can respond.

This truth also applies to emotional regulation and managing stress. When you get stressed out, there's usually a ramping-up period. Not always, but often. A lot of stress we deal with culminates. It builds and grows to a point that eventually becomes overwhelming and unmanageable. However, suppose you learn to listen to your body's cues. In that case, you can treat stress similarly to coming down with a cold. If you know your signs, you can intervene and ward off overwhelm and use your vagus nerve to flexibly regulate and calm.

Know Your Signs

Do you know your stress "tells"? What are the signs and symptoms that your body sends to inform you that you're getting overwhelmed and worked up? Those signs and symptoms are indicators that you're getting activated, and it's time to throw your vagus nerve a lifeline and ward off an emotional catastrophe. Think about what you experience when you feel stressed out and dysregulated. Write down the symptoms you relate to using the outline below for inspiration. Add any additional symptoms you are aware of, even if they aren't noted here.

- Muscle tension

- Headaches

- Sleep disturbance

- Changes to appetite

- Cravings for food or substances

- Racing thoughts

- Excessive worry

- Irritability or anger

- Depression

- Anxiety or panic attacks

- A loss of interest in hobbies or relationships

- Problems with digestion

- Skin issues such as a flare of eczema or psoriasis

- Changes to your sex drive

- Racing heart

- Emotional or physical numbness

- Feeling jittery, restless, unable to sit still

- Difficulty concentrating

- Feeling disconnected from your body

- An urge to isolate

- Feeling checked out, spacey, or forgetful

- Hopelessness

- Changes to eye contact with others

- Loss of happiness and joy

- Obsessive thinking

- Nightmares

- Physical pain

- Feeling frozen, indecisive, uncertain

- Hair loss

- Increased use of addictive substances

- Increased or decreased energy

The next step is putting this knowledge into practice. Similar to getting sick, these signs are warning signals. They are opportunities to intervene. If you don't intervene, your stressed-out nervous system will continue to do just that...stress. But when you learn to listen, you can do something and change the outcome. Emotional dysregulation does not have to be an out-of-control experience. However, to change the outcome, you have to be able to identify the signs.

Suppose you noticed you were getting sick but decided to stay up all night working on a project, ate a bunch of fast food, and smoked a pack of cigarettes. In that case, you're setting yourself up for disaster. That cold now has the power to morph into something really sucky, like pneumonia or bronchitis. If, instead, you listened to your body's cues, then you can make good decisions to improve your fate. If you get a good night's sleep, drink lots of fluids, and rest, the outcome will be significantly better. Your choices allow you to improve your recovery time, decrease the likelihood of serious illness, and prevent symptoms from worsening. This same logic applies to how you manage stress.

Let's say you notice you're getting stressed and overwhelmed, but you make those same choices: stay up all night, eat a bunch of fast food, and smoke a bunch of cigarettes. In that case, it's a guarantee you're going to feel emotionally terrible tomorrow. You cannot feed your nervous system poison and expect it to work in your favor. But suppose you identify your stress signals and prioritize your needs with rest, nutrition, and emotion regulation strategies. In that case, you might actually feel better tomorrow. Why? You notice what your nervous system needs and decide to work with it rather than against it.

Choices have consequences, and how we react to stress is no exception. But to better your odds in the face of stress, you have to know your pressure points and your signs. That awareness empowers you to make the choices that benefit you, your loved ones, and everyone around you. Awareness opens the doors for action and intervention.

Highlights and Takeaways

- Stress and emotional overwhelm are inevitable parts of life, but we are not doomed to become victims of them.

- The nervous system is front and center when it comes to regulating emotions. Polyvagal theory will help you understand how your nervous system works and offer empowering strategies for living a more balanced and regulated life.

- The vagus nerve is the mind-body connection that influences emotional wellness. It connects to several places in the body, including the inner ear, face, throat, vocal cords, lungs, heart, and digestive organs.

- The vagus nerve plays a major role in stress responses and emotional well-being.

- When the vagus nerve is activated in response to danger or stress, it can lead to a host of physical and emotional forms of suffering.

- Pressure points are triggers or stressors that activate stress responses.

- Identifying your unique "pressure points" or sources of stress is key to applying polyvagal theory to your life.

- Being mindful of bodily stress signals can help us intervene early to ward off emotional overwhelm.

Chapter 2

What Is Polyvagal Theory?

What the heck is polyvagal theory, and why does it matter to you? What's the buzz about, and how can learning this scientific model benefit your life? As you are reading a self-help book, I assume you are searching for ways to better yourself. You're hoping to get some tips to manage stress, find more peace and joy, heal from difficult life experiences, and reach your peak level of performance. Polyvagal theory will help you with all of that. So yes. It matters to you.

Whatever your goal is in reading this book, it has something to do with your nervous system. You may say, "No. I did not pick up this book thinking about my nervous system." But I promise you, whatever your goals may be, your nervous system has a central role in turning them into a reality.

Your nervous system informs, filters, perceives, and interprets every moment of your day. Every emotion, thought, behavior, movement, sneeze, fart, cough, and laugh is produced by your nervous system along with many other bodily systems. Your nervous system interacts with every system of your body and, in doing so, keeps you alive. The trillion cells in this system communicate through neurons using electrical pulses, neurotransmitters, and hormones. Whether you get a good or bad night's sleep, your nervous system has a role. When you feel hungry or full, that's your nervous system. When you look into your dog's eyes and feel those warm fuzzies, that's your nervous system. When you feel happy—nervous system. When you feel sad—nervous system. Anxiety, depression, joy, love, sorrow, pain…it's ALL your nervous system. You are the product of all the electrical currents and neurotransmitters pulsing between your neurons, held together by a suit of skin.

Given that your nervous system is at the heart of everything, it will play a major role in turning your self-help aspirations into reality. A healthy and resilient nervous system will be one of your greatest assets for achieving your goals, finding more peace and fulfillment, and living a happy life. So, learning how to understand your nervous system, what it needs, and how to befriend it is going to do you oodles of good on your quest for more balance and less stress. Knowledge is power, and learning how to work with your nervous system is an overlooked super-power. And the only thing you need to unlock that power is the desire to learn and try.

Polyvagal theory helps you achieve exactly this. Although this theory may feel dense and scientific at first, you will find that learning about the vagus nerve gives you priceless insights that lead you to have a true friendship with your neurobiology. Dr. Stephen Porges, a neuro-scientist and college professor, has dedicated years to developing this model. In 1969, Dr. Porges started researching heart rate and its impact on emotional well-being. Through his research, he discovered profound connections between heart rate, the vagus nerve, and mental and phys-ical wellness. Driven by his curiosity, he continued his investigations, gathering hypotheses and findings over several decades, ultimately forming what is now known as the polyvagal theory. Supported by many peer-reviewed articles and his highly respected books, this theory has been deemed the "science of safety." It explains how our nervous system responds to stress, sheds light on what we need to feel secure, and unveils how safety and connection play crucial roles in health and wellness.

It's important to note that your nervous system is a very large system, and stress affects lots of different neural pathways. Polyvagal theory focuses on the role the vagus nerve plays in emotional health and wellness. Still, it is not the only nerve or neurobiological structure that has a role in stressing out: not all stress responses and moments of emotional dysregulation are due to what your vagus nerve is doing. Your body is much more complex than that. Learning polyvagal theory, however, will give you a wealth of information and in-depth insight into how your nervous system functions. The vagus nerve is an incredibly important nerve for physical and emotional health, which has been demonstrated over and over in research. So, while it's not the only nerve that has a role in your stress levels and emotions, it is perhaps one of the most influential.

Core Principles of Polyvagal Theory

Polyvagal theory provides a framework for learning about your vagus nerve. It offers a wealth of information for understanding how and why you experience stress and what you need to diminish its negative effects. While the model has a lot of depth, and it is easy to get lost in the neuroscience of it all, you don't need to be an expert neuroscientist to apply its wisdom to your life. I'll do my best to simplify complex concepts into easy-to-digest nuggets and self-help strategies.

Let's dive in and explore some of the key components of the theory but keep things approachable and relatable. If you want an in-depth understanding of polyvagal theory and you enjoy geeking out on academic neuroscience, I recommend you dive into Porges's books and academic research articles.

1. **Poly-vagal:** First and foremost, polyvagal theory is called "polyvagal" because it describes the nerves that make up the vagus nerve. That's right, your vagus nerve isn't just one nerve: it has two branches of nerves that contain lots of nerve fibers. Porges named his model "polyvagal" because the theory is about how this bundle of nerves influences so many things.

2. **The "automatic" nervous system:** The theory explains how the vagus influences the *autonomic nervous system*. There are two "mini" branches of the autonomic nervous system, called sympathetic and parasympathetic, and together these systems make up the autonomic nervous system.

   The autonomic nervous system is reactive or "automatic." It responds to stimuli and stress automatically without conscious awareness. It is programmed to be reactive because it plays a big role in saving your life in times of danger. Thanks to genetics and evolution, your autonomic system comes prepro- grammed with survival strategies. These are commonly referred to as *fight-flight-freeze-faint* responses. The vagus nerve plays a significant role in turning those defenses on and off.

3. **Neuroception:** Your "automatic" nervous system is sensitive to the stimuli you come into contact with. It relies on a process called *neuroception*, which stands for *perception without aware- ness*, to decide if things in your environment are safe or danger- ous. Those pressure points you identified in chapter 1 are things your neuroception identifies to be dangerous, threaten- ing, or unpleasant. Your nervous system is constantly on the lookout for signs of danger because its number one priority is survival. Anything it perceives as potentially threatening or dangerous can cause your vagus nerve to activate defensive survival strategies or stress responses.

4. **The power of relationships:** Polyvagal theory also emphasizes the power of connection and interpersonal relationships. Dr. Porges discovered that the vagus nerve plays a role in creating safe bonds with other people and even animals. Without the vagus nerve, we'd be unable to form functional relationships.

    Connection is necessary for health and wellness. Healthy, supportive, loving relationships are, in fact, one of the most important things we need to thrive. Does that mean you need to become an extrovert with tons of besties? No. But one or two really safe, supportive relationships with other humans or animals truly does wonders for your mind and body. Just as a plant needs sunlight to grow, your nervous system needs con- nection to thrive. Polyvagal theory explains the significance of relationships for health and wellness and the role the vagus nerve plays in creating safety with each other.

5. **The importance of evolution:** Polyvagal theory also examines the role that evolution has played in the development of the

nervous system we all have today. Over millions of years, our autonomic nervous system has evolved from a system with few survival tactics to a system able to mobilize and fight or flee to one that's capable of feeling safe and forming social bonds—the nervous system we have today. This transformation has taken place over 500 million years. Mother Nature is smart and has given us a diverse array of survival strategies (fight, flight, freeze, and faint) along with the capacity to experience restful and restorative states.

The Basic Exercise

Throughout this book, you will continue to learn exercises that stimulate your vagus nerve to promote more peace, wellness, and balance in your life. Some have accompanying exercises that can be found at http://www.newharbinger.com/54124.

There are numerous ways to tap into your vagus nerve and regulate your neurobiology, though the basic exercise is one that uses the head and eyes to access the vagus nerve's calming properties. This exercise is best learned while lying down, though you can also practice from a seated position. It is a physical strategy to increase blood flow to the brainstem, positively affecting the vagus (Rosenberg 2017). It works by influencing muscles and nerves behind your eyes and in your neck. This exercise takes less than five minutes, making it a quick go-to when you need some regulation.

Lie down on your back.

Interlace your fingers.

Bring your hands behind your head and rest your head in your interlaced hands. If you can't do this, rest your head in one hand.

Let go of tension in your shoulders, arms, and neck. Keep your body relaxed and loose.

Keep your head centered and still, and shift your gaze to the right.
Find a place to hold your gaze that doesn't strain your eyes. You can
do this with your eyes open or closed.

Hold your gaze there until you notice a yawn, a swallow, a sigh, or a
deep breath. This may happen in a few seconds or in a few minutes.

NOTE: If it doesn't happen, adjust your gaze up, down, or look closer
or further away. Be sure not to strain your eyes. Experiment with your
gaze and wait for the shift.

Bring your eyes back to the center and pause for a few seconds.

Repeat numbers 5 and 6 on the left side.

Return your gaze to the center, release your hands, and rest. Check
in and notice any shifts in your physical or emotional state.

Practicing the basic exercise can produce a sense of calm and help you feel more regulated. After practicing this, you might also discover that you have more movement in your neck and shoulders. The shifts are typically subtle but meaningful.

The Wealth of Neurological Health

Emotional health is a product of physical health, and physical health is a product of emotional health. Though a lot of people see emotional health as separate from physical health, the two are, in fact, intimately intertwined. Thoughts, feelings, and emotions are not fluffy, woo-woo, made-up constructs. They are physical experiences produced by your physical body.

If we acknowledge that physical and emotional health are one and the same, our perspective changes. Feelings and emotions aren't made-up ideas, things to stuff down or just "get over," but rather physical symptoms caused by your nervous system. Knowing this, you might interact with them differently. Emotions are simply the product of neurophysiological functioning. We likely wouldn't tell a friend to "get over" an asthma attack or tell ourselves to "suck it up, buttercup" when we have the stomach flu. So why would we think we could just "get over" an anxiety attack or that a depressive episode is all in your head? They're all manifestations of physical "stuff" happening in our bodies.

Like the rest of your body, your nervous system and vagus nerve need to be cared for. If you don't care for your body, it won't optimally function. It's that simple. And if your nervous system isn't cared for, coping skills and therapeutic techniques won't work. Polyvagal theory emphasizes that the vagus nerve has tremendous healing potential when we use it for good. We can unlock the healing power of the nervous system by using the knowledge of neurobiology to bolster and support us. However, you can also engage in habits and behavior patterns that cause your nervous system to work against you. Your nervous system isn't a machine. It's a living, breathing, growing, and changing part of your body, and it needs resources and nutrients to optimally function. When we engage in practices that promote and support a healthy nervous system, we work with our neurobiology rather than against it.

Improving your stress management skills and learning to unleash the power of your vagus nerve for good starts with examining your health practices. What are you "feeding" your nervous system, and how is that hindering or helping you? We have to get real with ourselves and identify what we're doing well and where we need growth. Only then can we identify a path forward.

My Health Practices

If you want the exercises in this book to have an effect, it's important to prioritize your foundational health needs. Your vagus nerve is crucial to your overall well-being and requires adequate resources to function optimally. Basic health practices serve as the building blocks for a resilient nervous system. It's worth noting that good intentions alone won't guarantee results. Many factors can influence basic health practices like sleep and appetite, some of which may be out of your control. Caring for a newborn will absolutely impact your sleep, and having limited resources for nutritious food will pose barriers to using food as medicine. But no matter the circumstances, there's always something you can do, even if it's small, to positively impact your health and wellness.

There is no such thing as one-size-fits-all when it comes to health practices. Every body is different, with different needs and sensitivities. And there are a lot of factors that affect a person's ability to engage in health practices. Income, exposure to pollution and hazardous chemicals, access to clean water, access to good health care, and genetics, are a few among many others. This section of the book is not meant to overlook the socioeconomic inequalities that exist throughout the world but to speak to neurobiological facts.

Research identifies that there are a few common variables that can significantly improve neurological health for everyone. These factors include sleep, nutrition, and social connection. No matter your situation, it's important to pay attention to these factors as you consider ways to help your nervous system help you.

In this exercise, we will explore health practices that promote optimal vagal health. You are not expected to be a champion in all of these areas, and there are likely unique factors, as mentioned above, that influence how you engage with these practices. Approach this assessment with curiosity and an open mind, without guilt or shame, and look for opportunities to make small improvements. Every little bit counts in service of having more resources available to you to manage stress. And that's exactly what the following domains offer your nervous system: resources.

Self-rate each health domain on a scale of 0 to 10, with 0 being the absolute worst and 10 being the absolute best.

Sleep: Sleep is the foundation of health and wellness. It is vital for healthy metabolism, memory consolidation, and physical restoration (Ohlmann et al. 2009). Sleep is the most important activity we do on a daily basis. It's even more important than diet and exercise! It is highly regenerative and crucial for optimal physical, psychological, and neurological functioning. Most of us need six to eight hours of sleep per night. Some of us need more, and some of us need less. A dark, quiet, cool room is ideal for sleep. It's best to get to sleep quickly and stay asleep for most or all of the night. (Parents of newborns…sorry to remind you of what you are desperately longing for right now.) If you don't get enough sleep, you are prone to illness, heart disease, cancer, cognitive impairment, memory decline, weight gain, diabetes, and accidents. If you don't get enough sleep, it is a guarantee that your physical and emotional health will suffer, and your ability to work with your vagus nerve will be significantly impaired.

0–10

Rate your sleep

Hydration: Most of the body is made up of water. So, of course, you need to drink enough of it to feel good (Carretero-Krug et al. 2021). Hydration supports every system of the body. It aids digestion, immune system functioning, muscle growth, energy, physical performance, weight management, the transportation of oxygen throughout the body, joint mobility, and kidney functioning. Hydration is also important for optimal heart health, memory, cognition, and emotion regulation (Ganio et al. 2011; Kempton et al. 2011)

Adults need around sixty-four ounces of water daily to stay hydrated. That's about eight glasses. This number can vary depending on age, weight, and activity level.

0–10

Rate your water intake

Diet: What you put into your body affects how your body functions. If we don't eat enough nutritious food full of protein, carbohydrates, and nutrients, our energy, sleep, mood, and physical wellness suffer. Living on processed food is like putting sugar into your gas tank. It just doesn't work. A nutritious diet includes fruits and vegetables, lean protein, and whole grains. High-processed food, alcohol, sugary snacks, and foods high in salt and saturated fat, if eaten regularly in excess, can negatively affect the nervous system. In addition to eating nutritious food, we need to eat *enough* of it. Each of us has a unique caloric intake requirement based on age, height, weight, and activity level. If we eat too much food, we can overwhelm our system. At the same time, if we are calorie deficient, our bodies don't have enough energy resources to get through the day.

There are many theories, approaches, and beliefs about what a nutritious diet looks like. I will not examine those here. Rather than thinking about foods as "healthy" versus "unhealthy," consider if what you're putting into your body is helping or hindering your stress management goals. There's nothing wrong with having a sweet treat or a salty snack. But if you live on foods that are known troublemakers and you rarely eat the foods that allow your body to thrive, it will be hard, or impossible, to improve your health and wellness. What you feed your body matters, and we must take this into consideration when it comes to emotional health.

0–10
Rate your diet

Safe, supportive connection: The nervous system thrives in the presence of safe, healthy, supportive connections with others. We are wired to connect and form bonds. When we feel safe and seen by others, our body produces neurochemicals that promote wellness. Whether you're an introvert or an extrovert, you need relationships. Good relationships are medicinal. On the flip side, toxic, chaotic, and unsafe relationships are incredibly harmful to the nervous system.

A handful of safe, supportive relationships with other people or animals can do wonders for your nervous system. Think about the important people and animals in your life. Who do you identify as supportive and safe, consistent and dependable, loving and caring, nurturing and compassionate? Who are the people and animals you can be yourself with, who don't cause you shame or guilt, who treat you with respect and kindness regularly, and bring more good than bad into your life?

0–10
Rate the quality of your relationships

Now that you've taken a baseline, identify one concrete, realistic thing you can do in the next week in each category to improve your score. Write down your goals and place them somewhere you will see them regularly. Maybe that's your bedside table, your bathroom mirror, or an app on your phone. Create small goals you feel confident you can achieve and bring them to the forefront of your mind with visual reminders. The more you remind yourself of your goals, the more likely it is that you will engage in the habits that will help you achieve them.

Here's some inspiration if you're struggling to find concrete, realistic goals:

- No scrolling in bed.
- Make your room more conducive to sleep with blackout curtains, a sound machine, or a fan.
- Drink a glass of water first thing in the morning.
- Eat one more piece of fruit per day.
- Make a coffee date with a friend or take your dog to the park.
- Say no to hanging out with that person who always creates drama.
- Listen with intention to your body's hunger cues.
- Avoid caffeine after 4 p.m.

Little changes in these areas can translate to big gains. You may not want to do some of these things. After all, fast food can sound way more appealing than taking time to cook a nutritious meal, and scrolling may feel more interesting than going to bed. But think of your health practices like taxes or going to the doctor. You never really want to do those things, but you do them to avoid the consequences that come from not doing them. And when it comes to health habits, the more you do them, the more you'll crave them, and eventually, they won't feel like work.

Autonomic Pathways and the Vagus Nerve

Your vagus nerve is part of your biology. If you don't engage with it or try to work with it, you miss out on a key resource for managing stress. Therefore, working with your vagus nerve and its functions can result in considerable benefits. You can learn to work with your vagus nerve by learning how it works along with techniques to stimulate it, producing desired results. When you practice skills that promote nervous system regulation, you are ultimately engaging your vagus nerve and your autonomic nervous system for your benefit. You are taking control back from the sometimes out-of-control experience of stress.

The vagus has a significant influence on what your autonomic nervous system does. Your autonomic nervous system is made up of three pathways, each producing specific emotional and physical responses. One of these pathways mobilizes you and produces fight-or-flight responses. Another pathway immobilizes you and can produce a freeze or shutdown response. And the third pathway is the just-right zone, where connection and balance live. Finding ways to intentionally work with these pathways can improve your ability to tolerate and process emotions and help you adapt to life changes (Park and Thayer 2014; Porges 2021).

In the upcoming chapters, we will dive into the principles of polyvagal theory that are most relevant to self-help. You'll discover a range of exercises that engage the power of your vagus nerve to ward off and manage stress. Some of the techniques covered will be useful for reducing overwhelm in the moment, and others will help you become more resilient in response to stress over time. As you progress, you'll expand your knowledge and understanding of not only the vagus nerve but also your neurobiology, gaining concrete skills to regulate stress levels.

A Note on Neurodivergence

Neurodivergence is a term that refers to folks with a nervous system wired a little differently than the "typical" wiring most medical and societal standards are based on. This can include (but is not limited to) people with autism, highly sensitive people, those with ADD, and those diagnosed with a mental illness. If you have a neurodivergent nervous system, learning about these autonomic pathways can sometimes feel confusing and exclusive. Let's address that right here because your experience matters and so does your nervous system!

Some diagnoses and conditions result from overwhelming, traumatic events that affect neurological functioning. Grief and trauma are two events that have profound impacts on our brain and neurobiology. Many other diagnoses have a biological underpinning to them. Some diagnoses are due to how your nervous system is uniquely wired based on genetics and early development. Other diagnoses may be due to a physical injury that impacts how your brain functions. And finally, some other diagnoses are due to an imbalance of neurochemicals or the structure of your brain. There are a lot of factors that influence how each person's system uniquely functions. Some of those factors are within our control, and some are not.

Neurodivergent presentations, such as ADD, ADHD, autism, bipolar disorder, psychotic disorders, and traumatic brain injuries, alter the "normative" functioning of the autonomic nervous system. The autonomic nervous system doesn't solely respond to stimuli. It also responds to neurochemicals and hormones and how you are physiologically put together. For someone with a neurodivergent diagnosis, atypical autonomic functioning may be a hallmark of that diagnosis. Sometimes, our autonomic nervous system behaves in certain ways because of brain chemistry, brain functioning, an injury, or a medical condition. Not every experience of dysregulation is caused by stress. Your nervous system is way more complicated than that.

This doesn't mean this book can't be helpful. Read this book through your unique, individual perspective. While all humans have similarities in how our nervous system functions, we also have unique differences. No matter how your nervous system works, we all experience and respond to stress. The tips and techniques in this book can be useful for anyone, whether you have a neurodivergent nervous system or not. Working with your vagus nerve benefits a host of physical and psychological conditions, including neurodivergent diagnoses! The techniques in this book won't cure a neurodivergent diagnosis through stress management techniques. But they can help you better manage stress and may even help you reduce some challenging symptoms associated with neurodivergence.

Highlights and Takeaways

- Polyvagal theory, developed by Dr. Stephen Porges, is a theoretical model that explains the functions of the vagus nerve and how the autonomic nervous system responds to stress. The theory sheds light on what we need for health and wellness, and it describes how safety and connection play crucial roles in emotional and physical well-being.

- Neuroception is a polyvagal term that stands for perception without awareness. Your nervous system is constantly looking for danger or alarm. It will activate survival and stress responses without your conscious awareness.

- Relationships are medicinal for the nervous system; the vagus nerve plays a key role in feeling safe and bonding with others.

- Emotional and physical health are intertwined. Taking care of your physical health is a means of taking care of your emotional health. Sleep, hydration, a nutritious diet, and safe relationships establish the foundation for wellness and resiliency.

- Polyvagal theory provides an instruction manual for understanding how and why we experience stress and what we need to diminish the negative effects of it.

- With skills and health practices, you can learn to influence your vagus nerve and decrease your stress responses.

Chapter 3

The Autonomic Nervous System

Your nervous system is like the world's busiest dance floor—constantly pulsing with electrifying energy. While the nervous system may seem like a minor aspect of your biology, it shapes your life in tremendous ways. Without your nervous system, you wouldn't feel feelings. You wouldn't have thoughts. You wouldn't have memories. It's mind blowing and humbling to think about how powerful the nervous system is and how it informs and influences every moment of our lives! Yet, we rarely think about it, what it's doing, and what it needs.

In neuroscience, the nervous system gets broken down into branches or sections. This makes it easier to study because otherwise, it's one huge, complex web of processes and functions. Different branches have different roles and jobs. For example, your brain and spinal cord are part of one branch, the central nervous system. You also have a branch known as the somatic nervous system, which controls muscles and movement. And there's even a part of your nervous system that controls the bacteria in your gut and the contraction of muscles in your stomach, known as the enteric nervous system. The autonomic nervous system is the focus of polyvagal theory. The vagus nerve is capable of engaging different pathways of your autonomic nervous system based on its influence on your heart. Your vagus nerve can pull the metaphorical strings on your autonomic nervous system like a puppeteer pulling the strings on a puppet. But instead of pulling strings, your vagus nerve uses your heart and a variety of neurochemicals to change your neurophysiological state.

The autonomic nervous system consists of two branches: sympathetic and parasympathetic. The sympathetic nervous system is a mobilizing pathway. It increases your heart rate and gives you energy to get through the day. When the sympathetic nervous system responds to stress or threat, the vagus nerve increases heart rate, leading to feelings such as anxiety, panic, fear, and irritability.

The parasympathetic branch is described in polyvagal theory as having two pathways termed ventral and dorsal. The ventral part of your parasympathetic nervous system is sometimes called the "social engagement system." When you feel calm, peaceful, or connected to others, you can thank your ventral vagal pathway for those experiences. The other part of the parasympathetic system is called the dorsal vagal pathway. This part of your nervous system has conservation qualities that allow your body to repair and regenerate. However, the dorsal vagal pathway can be recruited in defense, which leads to lethargy, hopelessness, depression, and feeling void of energy. In contrast, the sympathetic pathway is involved in movement, including play and defense. Think of the pathways as siblings with different adaptive qualities, all serving our adaptation in this dynamically changing world.

Each pathway comes with unique qualities. Together they give us humans a delightful rollercoaster of emotional experiences. These three pathways are all influenced by the vagus nerve. Additionally, these pathways can change their tone depending on whether you feel safe or threatened. They contribute to a balanced, flourishing life when you feel safe. But when you experience danger or stress, the vagus nerve moves these pathways to protect and defend you.

In this chapter, we will examine these pathways in depth. You will learn each pathway's physical and psychological qualities and how to decipher which pathway you're in. With this knowledge, you can use techniques to cue the pathway you need at the right time, leading to more power and control over your stress responses.

Autonomic Pathways

Your autonomic pathways are, metaphorically, like gears on a car. Just as a car can cruise or race, your neurobiology can also pulse at different speeds depending on which pathways are engaged. When we can use these pathways to intentionally shift our "speed," we feel like masters of the highway (aka our lives). But you might recall what it was like when you learned to drive. Learning to find the right speed to work the pedals and gears was a chaotic experience at first. Similarly, until you learn to maneuver the gears of your autonomic nervous system, things can feel a tad out of control.

Just like there are no good or bad gears on a car, there are no good or bad pathways. They are all needed and necessary. But, when we have little control over our nervous system or are flooded with stress and traumatic experiences, these pathways get stuck in survival and protection mode, leaving us feeling messy, emotionally imbalanced, and incredibly stressed. Like a car that won't move out of first gear, life is challenging when our autonomic pathways don't optimally function. The vagus nerve controls these pathways and can direct one pathway to take the lead over another.

Here are the three autonomic pathways and their general qualities:

1. **Ventral:** Qualities of this pathway include feeling balanced, calm, and regulated. It's the just-right Goldilocks zone in your nervous system.

2. **Sympathetic:** This pathway is our energizing and mobilizing pathway. It gives us access to energy and contributes to feeling motivated, playful, and attentive. When activated in response to fear or stress, it can lead us to feel anxious, worried, and tense.

3. **Dorsal:** This pathway is one of stillness and immobilization. When activated in the context of safety and connection, we may feel calm, still, tired, and tranquil. However, when activated in response to stress, it can take on the qualities of numbness, depression, hopelessness, loneliness, and even dissociation.

Context Matters

Your autonomic pathways are the ultimate multitaskers, working behind the scenes to equip you with the neurobiological mojo necessary for conquering the day. When you feel safe, these pathways contribute to wellness and happiness, but when we're stressed, these pathways move to safeguard and shield us. The vagus nerve activates these pathways in response to danger and safety.

Your nervous system constantly assesses your environment, determining whether something is safe or unsafe, pleasant or unpleasant, friend or foe. If something is deemed unpleasant or dangerous, your pathways kick into defensive mode to protect you from potential harm. The telltale signs of stress, such as muscle tension, anxiety, worry, rumination, exhaustion, and loss of motivation, are all made possible by autonomic pathways acting out of defense. When we get stuck in defensive states for too long, our nervous system feels chaotic, our physical health takes a hit, and our relationships get dramatic and messy.

Context matters for your autonomic pathways. When these pathways are active in the context of safety, they reward us with rich life experiences. When we feel safe and peaceful, we have the energy to get through the day and are able to rest when it's time to rest. But if these pathways get activated in response to danger or threat, they move us into the survival strategies of fight, flight, freeze, or faint. It's all about the context and what these pathways are responding to. Like a chameleon can change its colors to match its surroundings, these pathways can change their functioning based on environmental cues of danger and safety. Learning how your pathways respond to cues of safety versus cues of danger will unlock a treasure trove of personal insights for managing stress and living a more balanced life.

Your Autonomic Blueprint

Unlocking the mysteries of the three autonomic pathways has revolutionized my perspective on stress and how to combat it. Knowing the unique characteristics of each pathway, I can more easily identify when stress is creeping in and take steps to avoid it from reaching an intolerable, critical level. I've become a pro at recognizing when I'm on the edge of overwhelm, when my stress levels are skyrocketing, and when it's time to tap out and reset. The autonomic nervous system works on autopilot, responding to stimuli without us even realizing it. Unfortunately, many of us are clueless about what our nervous systems are up to throughout the day. While you might be able to identify when you're at your breaking point, most of us struggle to track the escalation and buildup of stress. But once you learn how to spot the warning signs, you'll have a greater chance to intervene before things get out of hand.

Your nervous system has a unique blueprint for how it responds to safety and danger. It's like your own personal code that signals when overwhelm is on the horizon. Your body sends messages through subtle symptoms, which can become your allies for managing and beating stress. Your nervous system gives you signs and clues for what it needs and when it's overwhelmed. Learning to identify those signs allows you to respond and take charge of stress rather than it take charge of you. But first, you have to create your autonomic blueprint and learn to read the language of your neurobiology.

I first learned how to create a blueprint of my nervous system through the work of Deb Dana, a pioneer in the polyvagal world (Dana 2018). In the following exercise, you will get introspective and learn the telltale signs of each pathway. Charting and learning your autonomic blueprint will allow you to attune to your body and neurobiology, a required step to integrating polyvagal theory into your life. Let's get to it.

The Ventral Pathway

Meet your ventral pathway. Ventral is one of two pathways that make up your parasympathetic nervous system. Ventral is where health, wellness, restoration, and connection live. It is the Goldilocks zone—the "just right" zone, the "everything is groovy" zone. When ventral takes the reins, we tend to be our best selves.

When our nervous system isn't bombarded with danger signals, stressors, or threats, we can get cozy with our ventral pathway. But if we become flooded with fear, we can quickly lose our connection to this pathway. Learning polyvagal theory will help you maintain that pre-cious connection to ventral even when life gets challenging. It is, in fact, your capacity to stay tethered to this pathway in times of extreme stress that will ultimately help you achieve more emotional balance and experience challenges with greater ease. Maintaining a connection to ventral reduces the consequences we sometimes create for ourselves when we are emotionally reactive or spun out from stress.

There are specific emotional and physical qualities that accompany the ventral path. In ventral, we can connect to others, we are interested in relationships, and we are able to create healthy bonds with people and animals. We feel hopeful about the future, motivated, and playful here. This is the pathway of emotional balance, where we are able to tolerate stress, cope, and feel peace and ease. Ventral supports our ability to learn as it fosters curiosity and creativity and is the pathway that allows us to best retain new information. Digestion, circulation, heart rate, blood pressure, respiration, and even the immune system work best when we're well connected to ventral. And no surprise, this is also the zone of optimal, restful sleep cycles.

Here's a summarized list of ventral qualities:

Emotional Qualities of Ventral

Playful	Calm and balanced	Regulated
Confident	Curious and open	Motivated
Hopeful	Rested	Energized
Attentive and alert	Connected to others	Engaged in hobbies

Physical Qualities of Ventral

Regulated heartbeat and breathing	Restful sleep	Regulated blood pressure
Optimal immune functioning	Restful sleep	Enough energy to get through the day
Optimal immune functioning	The body feels just right, not stiff with worry or numb with despair	Engagement in eye contact with others
Regulated appetite without intolerable cravings or urges	Optimal digestive functioning	Regulated body temperature

Note that this list is not exhaustive. Use it as inspiration; now let's create your ventral blueprint.

On a piece of paper, jot down your signs of ventral. What are your emotional and physical markers of ventral? Consider the following when you're connected to ventral:

- Mood

- Thoughts and beliefs

- Quality of sleep

- Digestion, appetite, and cravings

- Pain and tension

- Hobbies and interests

- Relationships

- Use of mind-altering substances

- Sex drive

- Relationships with friends, families, and strangers

- School and work performance

- Anything else that stands out to you

Now, let's get a bit more connected with this pathway. Answer the following:

- What color aligns with ventral?

- What song or music genre aligns? What would ventral's walk-out song be, like a baseball player walking up to bat?

- What is a symbol or image that aligns with ventral?

- Finally, what do you want to call this pathway? Name it in your own words. Some examples include "aligned," "regulated," or "in the zone."

The Sympathetic Pathway

Next up, your sympathetic pathway. This is a mobilizing pathway where energy and action live. The energizing properties of this pathway allow us to feel motivated, alive, energized, and playful. But if this pathway gets recruited in response to fear, threat, or stress, it changes its tune: in the presence of stress, the sympathetic pathway is where anxiety, panic, fear, and anger live. When the sympathetic circuit responds to danger cues, we experience the qualities of fight or flight. We feel hypervigilant, worked up, on edge, jittery, and restless. We might ruminate, experience obsessive thinking, and find it difficult to concentrate and retain information. We can experience muscle tension, an increase in pain, heart palpitations, shallow breathing, and heightened blood pressure. All of those qualities are helpful if you need to run away from danger or fight off an attacker. But suppose you don't actually need fight-or-flight responses to survive a stressor like a frustrating and annoying work meeting. In that case, those qualities can feel like overkill.

Here's a summarized list of sympathetic qualities in response to fear and danger:

Emotional Qualities of Sympathetic

Anxiety, panic, and worry	Racing thoughts and rumination	Anger and irritability
Nightmares	Catastrophizing	Flashbacks
Rehashing an experience over and over	Overwhelm	Distraction and difficulty concentrating
Struggling to connect with others	Difficulties listening and following conversations	Obsessive and compulsive behaviors
Talking too fast	Feeling on edge	Feeling like you're too much, unstable, or a loose wire

Physical Qualities of Sympathetic

Racing heart	Rapid, shallow breathing	Increased blood pressure
Adrenaline dump	Feeling jittery and on edge	Weight loss
Muscle tension	Headaches	Loss of appetite
Unable to sleep, waking frequently, restless sleep	Increased sensitivity to sensory stimuli such as sounds, smells, and textures	Restlessness, can't sit still, an urgency to move

Now, just as you did for your ventral pathway, write out your specific sympathetic blueprint when this pathway is activated in response to cues of danger and stress. Use the same reflection questions to create your blueprint.

Jot down your signs of sympathetic. What are your emotional and physical markers of this mobilizing path? Consider the following:

- Mood
- Thoughts and beliefs
- Quality of sleep

- Digestion, appetite, and cravings

- Pain and tension

- Hobbies and interests

- Relationships

- Use of mind-altering substances

- Libido and sex drive

- Relationships with friends, families, and strangers

- School and work performance

- Anything else that stands out to you

Answer the following:

- What color aligns with this pathway?

- What song or music genre goes along with sympathetic? What is sympathetic's walk-out song?

- What is a symbol or image that goes along with sympathetic?

- Finally, what do you want to call this pathway?

The Dorsal Pathway

Last but not least, meet dorsal, the pathway of immobilization. When dorsal is activated in the absence of fear or danger, it allows us to sit still, sleep, and rest. You need dorsal to enjoy the calmer, quieter moments of life. But if dorsal gets recruited because of fear or danger, it can cause us to withdraw and shut down. The dorsal pathway is where hopelessness, depression, despair, and shutdown live. In dorsal, we feel isolated and disconnected from others, and we lose interest in life. We lack motivation, energy, and desire. Our body goes into an extreme state of protection as it prepares to potentially sustain a serious emotional or physical injury. We turn inward like a turtle closing up its shell or check out. Fainting is one example of an extreme dorsal response to a threat. Feeling numb, disconnected from your body, and dissociated are also made possible by dorsal activation. Those could be great survival tactics if fighting and fleeing aren't options. But those extreme responses aren't helpful in many situations. After all, passing out in the conference room because your boss is working your last nerve isn't the best strategy.

Here are some of the unique characteristics of the dorsal pathway:

Emotional Qualities of Dorsal

Depression and Despair	Sadness and Loneliness	Numbness and flat emotions
Disorientation	Helplessness	Dissociation
Loss of desire to connect	Feeling dead inside	Flat affect
Loss of interest in activities, people, work/school, and/or life.	A desire to isolate	Sluggish thinking

Physical Qualities of Dorsal

Feeling depleted and exhausted	A desire to sleep more than you need	Difficulties animating your face
Low blood pressure	Slow heart rate	Slow breathing
Physical numbness .	Feeling tired/exhausted	Weight gain
Cravings and increased appetite	Slow digestion	Difficulties urinating or making a bowel movement

As you did for ventral and sympathetic, create your unique blueprint for the dorsal pathway:

- Mood

- Thoughts and beliefs

- Quality of sleep

- Digestion, appetite, and cravings

- Pain and tension

- Hobbies and interests

- Relationships

- Use of mind-altering substances

- Libido and sex drive

- Relationships with friends, families, and strangers

- School and work performance

- Anything else that stands out to you

Answer the following:

- What color aligns with this pathway?

- What song or music genre goes along with dorsal? What is dorsal's walkout song?

- What is a symbol or image that goes along with dorsal?

- Finally, what do you want to call this pathway? Name it in your own words.

Blended Pathways

Your system is rarely governed by just one pathway. More typical is a blend of pathways. Just like blending primary colors creates new colors, blending autonomic pathways creates additional neurological experiences.

Ventral + Sympathetic = Play + Performance

When ventral blends with sympathetic, we tend to feel energized but safe at the same time. With ventral being part of the concoction, we feel regulated, balanced, curious, and open, with vigor and energy. Consider the difference between feeling excited and energized versus anxious and afraid. Both require the sympathetic pathway, but the mobilizing energy changes its properties depending on whether you feel safe or unsafe. You might feel this blended state when you're playing with your dog or child, when you are working out at the gym, or when you're playing a game with friends. In those situations, you hopefully have enough cues of safety that your pathways aren't reacting out of fear, which allows your sympathetic pathway to lend mobilizing properties without engulfing you in a fight-or-flight response. If it weren't for that connection to ventral, the next time you got all excited on game night, you might run out the door screaming in terror or break dishes in a fit of rage.

Ventral + Dorsal = Stillness

When ventral is blended with dorsal qualities, we feel still, quiet, and chill. With ventral part of the mix, we're able to feel safe and calm while also feeling still in the presence of dorsal. With enough connection to ventral and safety, this blended experience lets us immobilize but not go to the extreme side of dorsal depression, despair, and hopelessness. When dorsal is able to add to the mixture, in the context of safety, we can lounge on the couch and watch a movie. We might fall asleep in a massage or at the end of a yoga class. We're able to snuggle with a loved one or pet, being fully immersed in the experience. If it weren't for the maintained connection to ventral, you'd get cozy on the couch and suddenly find yourself in a depressed, existential crisis. Or you'd get a massage and walk out feeling hopeless and worse than when you walked in. In these examples, you have enough connection to ventral to feel safe, but the addition of dorsal allows your body to deeply relax and immobilize.

Sympathetic + Dorsal = Freeze

Freeze is a response you have probably heard of before. It's a common survival tactic. Think of a bunny that you approach in the yard that freezes in the grass. Freeze presents with muscle tension and mobilizing energy. The sympathetic pathway gives an urge to mobilize, run away, or fight back while dorsal adds an immobilizing ingredient. Freeze is the mixed experience of having a lot of tension in the body yet being unable to move. Freezing is a useful strategy when you have to hide or remain very, very quiet in the face of danger. This mixture of tense, mobilizing energy, along with cautious immobilization in the presence of danger or threat, is the blended state of freeze. The blending of these two pathways gives you a whole extra survival strategy. This is often the blended state people experience when they're stuck in procrastination, ambivalence, or even the challenging experience of urgently wanting to take action but not being able to act.

Name Your Blended Pathways

Let's explore these blended pathways from your own lived experience and name them in your own words.

Ventral + Sympathetic

I call the state of feeling safe and *energized* _____.

Ventral + Dorsal

I call the state of feeling safe and *immobilized* _____.

Sympathetic + Dorsal

I call the state of feeling afraid, compelled to act, but unable to move or make a decision, _____.

Highlights and Takeaways

- You have three autonomic pathways, and the vagus nerve plays a significant role in how these pathways present in your life.

- The autonomic pathways include the ventral, sympathetic, and dorsal. Each pathway has associated physical, emotional, and social characteristics.

- Each pathway is necessary for life. When activated in response to danger or stress, they take on protective and defensive qualities.

- The dorsal pathway is a pathway of immobilization. Numbness, depression, and shutdown live here if this pathway is recruited in response to danger.

- The sympathetic pathway is a mobilizing pathway. Anxiety, fight and flight, and anger live here if this pathway is recruited in response to danger.

- The ventral pathway is your "social engagement" pathway. It is the just right zone where you feel balanced and well.

- Autonomic pathways can blend and create a diverse array of experiences. Freeze, play, and stillness are all examples of blended pathways.

- Understanding these pathways forms the basis for working with your autonomic nervous system stress responses and creating more emotional balance in your life.

Chapter 4

Neuroception

The nervous system's most important job is keeping you alive. One of the ways it does this is by making predictions about your survival needs. It has some very clever and sophisticated ways it monitors safety, makes predictions, and responds with calculated defenses. It is wired with the power of your autonomic pathways, recruited to defend, to protect you from imminently dangerous things like a poisonous snake, someone attacking you, or a burning building.

But sometimes it applies the same defensive strategies for life-or-death situations to day-to-day stressors. It can mistake something to be dangerous that isn't like your email inbox or a conversation with a loved one. While those emails and relationships might be challenging, they aren't life-threatening. I'm sure you can agree that the work deadline is not the same threat level as a burning building and doesn't require a five-alarm fire type of response from your autonomic nervous system. But your nervous system isn't logical. If left unchecked, the same protective bodily responses that get activated for imminent danger can get activated for minor stressors. No wonder stress feels so overwhelming!

Your nervous system is a loyal companion that always has your back. It prioritizes your survival above everything else. Even if it gets confused about what is and isn't imminently dangerous. It protects and predicts through a process called *neuroception*. Neuroception is an important term from polyvagal theory that stands for detection without awareness (Porges 2017).

Your system unconsciously scans everything you encounter for potential danger. This process of constantly checking out whether something is dangerous or not is neuroception. If neuroception detects something dangerous, your vagus nerve engages the protective functions of your autonomic pathways. Neuroception is not a conscious, logical process. It is predictive and reactive. Sometimes, its assessment is spot on, and sometimes, it can get us caught up in unnecessary emotional reactions. The rush of energy it activates in response to a car swerving into your lane is helpful. That jolt of mobilization coming from the sympathetic pathway makes you quickly react and potentially avoid an accident. However, that same rush of energy in response to your toddler's meltdown at the store is not so helpful.

Neuroception works by scanning three environments: stimuli in your external environment, feelings and sensations you experience within your body, and cues you pick up on from other creatures (people and critters) you come into contact with. This sophisticated system is programmed with information to quickly assess and predict, without your conscious awareness, whether something is safe or dangerous. If it senses something could be dangerous or threatening, autonomic pathways are activated to protect and defend. This can leave you swept away in a reactive, unpleasant, and overwhelming emotional experience that can lead to a lot of upset and distress in your life if the response is greater than the situation calls for.

The things that cue danger to your nervous system may be apparent or subtle. A pan on fire on the stove is undoubtedly a blazing sign of danger. But did you know that neuroception might also interpret someone's tone of voice, a smell, a crooked picture, or the lighting in a room to be a threat? Even though your brain might recognize that overhead lights do not threaten your survival, neuroception might say, "I don't like this. This makes me uneasy. It feels uncomfortable and, therefore, might be a threat." Considering these tiny nuances of neuroception, you might begin to understand how neuroception can be a key player in unwanted stress responses, leading to overwhelm.

A few years ago, I was browsing the ice cream aisle at the grocery store when I heard a loud pop. The noise caught my attention, and my neuroceptive processes perked up to assess the situation. *Was that a gun?* I wondered. I stood frozen in the freezer aisle, trying to quickly assess my safety. My heart rate sped up. I held my breath. Images of the mass shooting that had taken place the week before in a grocery store in my community ran through my mind. Flashes of a personal experience related to gun violence also started running through my mind.

My nervous system was alert, trying to make predictions and help me survive. I became acutely aware of all of the stimuli, sounds, smells, and people in the store at that moment. My brain was trying to process environmental data at warp speed. Additionally, my brain was sifting through all of the information it had about guns, using that information to make predictions. All of that information was preparing me to respond in a way that would support my odds of survival.

Some teenagers suddenly walked into the aisle. They were clearly goofing around. One of them had found some bubble wrap and was popping it in one of the other kid's ears. *Pop* went the bubble wrap while the victim of the hoax playfully punched their friend on the shoulder. "Oh," I thought. "It's just these kids goofing around. I'm safe. No gun." My heart rate slowed and my breathing returned to normal, so I tried to refocus on choosing an ice cream flavor.

I recognized at that moment that my automatic response to that startling noise was made possible because neuroception was doing its job. My system tuned into a sound that could have been a cue of danger, instantly preparing me with lots of energy in case I needed to run or fight. Even though there was no threat, my autonomic nervous system was primed and ready for action. I had been in a state of freeze until the moment I realized I was safe. My body was mobilized, ready to act, yet I was immobilized while I further assessed my surroundings. Neuroception had instantly told my vagus nerve what to do and which autonomic pathways I needed to be ready to respond.

Still standing in the ice cream aisle, I took some deep breaths in an effort to increase my connection to my ventral pathway. As I did so, I noticed I had an overall sense of unease in this grocery store. Moreover, I noticed those feelings seemed related to something more than that sound. "I really don't like this store. I wonder why that is," I thought. So, I got curious and started examining all the information neuroception was unconsciously appraising. I noticed that the store layout felt disorganized and crowded, which my nervous system didn't like. "Interesting," I thought. Remaining curious, I noticed I didn't like the bright overhead lights, how busy and crowded the store was, and I didn't know where the exits were. As I was checking out, I also noticed that the clerks at this store were not especially friendly. They didn't make eye contact, engage in conversation, or smile. While I certainly don't blame them for being burned out in a minimum wage job, the lack of connection influenced my neuroception and how I was feeling at the store.

I got home to find I had forgotten an essential ingredient for a recipe. So, I had to venture back out to the store. But this time, I went to a different store. Continuing with the theme of curiosity, I immediately noticed how much more my nervous system preferred the second store over the first. I preferred the layout of the second store. It was cleaner than the first store, well organized, and the aisles were wide and spacious. This store was less crowded, which my nervous system also preferred. Shoppers and staff at this store were friendlier. People smiled and made eye contact, and the staff were friendly with me and each other. They smiled and laughed and didn't seem to hate being at work. These were all bits of data that my nervous system quickly assessed and put value on. My neuroception appraised all of those cues as cues of safety, which allowed me to feel comfortable and at ease.

I had been to both of these stores multiple times before. But this was the first time I paid attention to how neuroception experienced each store. I became aware of the low-grade anxiety that would arise before I went grocery shopping at the first store. I realized that I dreaded shopping at the first store and typically walked out feeling stressed and overwhelmed. I felt at ease and calm while shopping at the second store. I experimented with this newfound awareness and shopped at the second grocery store for the next few weeks. I found that my typical dislike for grocery shopping changed. Shopping for groceries used to feel like an annoying chore, but now that I was going to this other store that my autonomic nervous system preferred, my dislike for grocery shopping reduced. Because I felt calm and safe at this store, I didn't feel the rise of dread on my drive, and I didn't walk out feeling overwhelmed and stressed.

I started listening to podcasts while shopping at the second grocery store. This is something I would never do at the first grocery because putting on headphones made it harder to hear things around me. As my nervous system already felt on guard at the first store, it definitely didn't like it if I tried to reduce my ability to hear potential danger by listening to a podcast! This was a new revelation I hadn't been aware of before. After a while, my nervous system started to see grocery shopping as an opportunity to be alone with my thoughts and take a break from the day! Yes. My nervous system turned grocery shopping into a coping skill. But that was only possible because I felt so safe at the second store, and I was able to notice the difference. Something as simple as grocery shopping can significantly impact our stress levels.

Take Neuroception Shopping

On your next run to the store, cozy up to your neuroceptive processes and learn your system's preferences. Any store will do. You might take this book with you or a copy of these questions to get curious as you study your own neurobiology. This exercise will help you learn to identify the external environmental cues that neuroception is evaluating.

1. Pick any store or outing. Experiment at multiple stores to notice differences in how your neuroception responds to stimuli.

2. Allow curiosity to guide you. Everyone has differences in their cues of danger and safety. There is no right or wrong.

3. Slowly scan your surroundings and tune into the plethora of stimuli that your senses are in contact with:

    Sight: What do you see? How would you describe the layout of the place you're in? Is it clean or cluttered? Organized or in disarray? Where are the exits? Is it crowded or empty? What's the lighting like? What colors do you notice?

    Smell: What does this place smell like?

Touch: What is the temperature? Is there airflow? What things can you touch, and what do they feel like? What does the ground or flooring feel like? What textures and physical sensations come along with this experience?

Sound: What sounds are you aware of? What do you hear in close proximity versus further away? Is it too loud, too quiet, or just right?

Taste: Do you have any tastes that accompany this space?

People: Are there people or animals around, and if so, how many? Too many, not enough, the right amount? How do you feel about what these people or animals are doing? What are your interactions like with the creatures in this space? How are creatures in this space interacting with each other?

4. Based on this new awareness, identify the things that feel uncomfortable, stressful, or threatening to your nervous system. You do not need an explanation or a reason. Sometimes, there is a deeper reason, and sometimes, cues just are what they are.

5. Identify the things that felt comfortable, appealing, or safe. You also don't need to have a why or an explanation. Just notice your preferences.

6. Were you aware of this information before this exercise? What stands out to you from this practice? Now that you've grown your awareness of the stimuli you've been reacting to, likely unconsciously until now, is there anything that surprises you? What are you aware of now that you weren't aware of before?

Your Personal Home Surveillance System

Neuroception is like a personal home surveillance system that constantly monitors the safety of your body. It's always on, looking for threats, ready to sound the alarm if it detects danger. Your nervous system and brain are capable of quickly assessing information, making predictions about your safety, and instantly cuing a defensive autonomic response. This strategy is highly effective when it comes to surviving imminent threats. But it can also be at the heart of overwhelming stress responses.

For comparison's sake, let's use a home security system as a metaphor. A home security system scans for threats and activates an alarm if it detects danger. Your home security system can monitor the doors, windows, smoke detectors, and even the outside perimeter of the house. It gets your attention if it senses an intruder outside or if a window breaks. It might contact 911 for you if it detects a fire. It does this all while you're asleep, away from home, or focused on other tasks.

The convenience of a home security system is that it takes the responsibility of constantly monitoring the safety of your home off of your to-do list. That security system means you don't have to constantly check the locks, worry about whether you closed the window, or fret about intruders breaking in. The system will let you know. This allows you to focus your time, energy, and resources on other tasks without sacrificing safety. It probably helps you sleep at night and allows you to enjoy your vacation while away.

Neuroception is a neurophysiological process similar to a home surveillance system. So long as your brain is functioning, it is using this process to monitor your safety. It is constantly on the lookout for danger or threat, just like a security system. It alerts you if something is wrong by activating autonomic defensive pathways. Depending on the threat and what it believes will be most helpful, it will instantly shift you into states of sympathetic mobilization or dorsal shutdown. From the bump in the night that wakes you up and makes you lie tense in your bed to the argument with your partner that makes you go flat inside and disengage...all of these responses are the outcome of neuroception assessing your situation.

This incredible safety system operates outside of your conscious, logical awareness. Why? Because thinking time is surviving time. If you had to think about your safety 24/7, it would be hard to get anything done. You would have to do safety checks constantly. "Are there any rabid animals in this room trying to attack me? Is anything on fire? Is my body okay? Am I bleeding or having a heart attack? Is this person safe?" Without neuroception, you would have to consciously check the safety of your environment, your body, and the people you interact with. Constantly. Because you couldn't trust that your nervous system would identify, "Hey, that's dangerous," and react accordingly. That would be exhausting and make it impossible to be productive. Luckily, your nervous system does this work for you in the background without you having to spend conscious mental energy on it.

Here are some common ways neuroception can affect us:

- Imagine suddenly hearing a loud, unexpected noise from behind. What would you instinctively do? You would automatically turn your attention toward that sound to check on safety. Your senses gravitate toward that sound, and your mind might start instinctively running through explanations and predictions about that noise. Your system will prepare with a predicted response. "Did my cat knock something off a shelf? Is that my kid playing with a toy? Is someone in my house? Did a tree just fall on my roof? Was that a ghost?" might be some potential scenarios you run through. Suppose you find that everything is okay and you're safe. In that case, neuroception takes a chill pill, allowing your autonomic pathways to calm and move back toward a state of ventral. But suppose neuroception alerts you to something truly dangerous, like an intruder or a child climbing on something that could hurt them. In that case, your autonomic nervous system is revved up and ready to respond because neuroception has it on speed dial. You can spring into action because neuroception is a few steps ahead of you, and your body is ready to respond. This is an example of how neuroception monitors your *external environment*.

- Think about what it's like to come down with the common cold. You likely notice signs before things are really bad. You might notice a tickle in your throat, watery eyes, or a stuffy nose. Neuroception picks up on those signs before your conscious brain and says, "Hey! Your nose is kinda stuffy. You're getting sick." You might check your temperature or take a COVID test. Maybe you take some vitamins, drink extra fluids, or take medicine to prevent things from worsening. If neuroception didn't alert you to those symptoms, you would lose valuable time in managing your sickness. Whatever you decide to do, neuroception has to first identify that you're feeling sick and bring that awareness to your attention. Without that awareness, you have zero opportunity to intervene. This is one example of how neuroception scans your *physical body* for danger or threat.

- We've all had the experience of meeting someone new who gives us the heebie-jeebies. Right off the bat, they've got bad vibes radiating off them like heat from the sun. You're chatting with someone you've never met, and something inside says, "I don't like this person. I don't feel comfortable. Get away." Yet, consciously, you aren't sure why you feel that way. They haven't said or done anything offensive, yet something inside says "danger, danger." That's neuroception! Because neuroception happens outside of your awareness, it might pick up on cues of danger or threat that your conscious brain isn't aware of. For example, neuroception might have picked up on a certain tone of voice or lack of eye contact, which your nervous system perceives as questionable or dangerous. Yet your conscious, logical brain is completely unaware of this, or at least isn't aware as quickly as neuroception is. Next time this happens, try to trust that intuition, aka neuroception. It is usually spot on. This is an example of how neuroception scans the *people and animals* you come into contact with.

Neuroception is an amazing thing, and we definitely don't want to get rid of it! It has kept you alive so far. However, sometimes, this reactive and automatic process can make life challenging when it overreacts or misinterprets. There are times when neuroception cues a reaction that is greater than the situation calls for. It can overshoot sometimes. And there are times when neuroception completely misinterprets a situation, perceiving something to be safe when it's dangerous. When neuroception is unable to accurately assess stimuli, and we can't activate or deactivate autonomic defenses, life can get messy. We feel out of control, overwhelmed, and incredibly stressed when this happens. Therefore, developing an awareness of neuroception and understanding how your system responds to cues can bring some control to otherwise uncontrollable emotional experiences.

Danger Cues

We all have stress signals that alert our brains to potentially dangerous scenarios. Some are obvious, like an angry dog racing toward you or a funnel cloud forming overhead. Others are subtle and easily overlooked, like crooked pictures, someone who smells bad, or a piece of clothing that is uncomfortable and doesn't fit right. These signals can range from life-threatening to merely annoying.

In polyvagal theory, these cues are known as "danger cues." In polyvagal terms, danger cues aren't solely focused on things that pose an imminent threat. Those danger cues can be stimuli your system doesn't like or finds to be stressful, unpleasant, or threatening. So when you read the term "danger cues," which is central to this theoretical model, don't necessarily associate that with imminently life-threatening situations. That term can be used broadly and expansively and relates to any stimuli that activate defensive autonomic responses. For example, some of my danger cues that aren't about imminent threat include clutter, large crowds, and noisy environments. While none of those situations alone pose imminent danger to my survival, my neuroception can cue mobilizing anxiety and a desire to flee when I encounter them.

We humans share lots of danger cues in common. Most of us (not all of us) feel startled if we see a shark fin pop up next to us when we're in the ocean and quickly tense up when a car swerves in front of us. However, danger cues also vary because of our unique neurobiology and personal histories. For example, some individuals are annoyed by loud noises, while others find noisy environments calming. Some people feel overwhelmed in crowds and public places, and some find safety in the herd. Some people find eye contact and a warm smile inviting, while others may find them unsettling. Sometimes, preferences are based on past experiences that have been unsafe or traumatic. For example, many combat veterans I have worked with in my career find the sound of fireworks to be a danger cue. Understandably so. My cousin, who has autism and has never served in combat, doesn't like fireworks either. When we were little, he'd always stay inside on the Fourth of July and play the piano while the rest of us kids ran around setting off bottle rockets. His neuroception doesn't like fireworks because of how his nervous system is uniquely and respectfully wired. My clients, on the other hand, don't like fireworks because the sound reminds them of war. Sometimes, there's a personal story, and sometimes, it's just how Mother Nature made you. And either is okay.

Learn Your Cues

Learning your cues requires self-reflection and self-study. You can use the following exercise to help develop and expand your awareness of neuroception. You'll identify even more by regularly checking in with yourself and the state of your autonomic pathways. Because neuroception is a passive, often unconscious process, you will identify cues most successfully as you notice how you respond to people, places, things, and stimuli throughout the day. As neuroception is always on and always working (even when you sleep!), you can check in with it at any point during the day to get a sense of what it's reading and how that's influencing your current experience.

Do you prefer small or large groups?

What's your personal bubble size? With strangers, with loved ones, with pets, with coworkers, with family?

What kind of facial expressions and body language tend to make you feel safe and comfortable with someone? What expressions and body language make you feel uneasy or unsafe?

Do you prefer dim, natural, or bright lighting?

Do you prefer clutter, organized chaos, or meticulously organized spaces?

Are there certain smells you can't stand? Are there certain smells that make you feel peaceful?

Are there textures that make you cringe? Conversely, are there textures that you find soothing?

Are there certain people or personality traits that activate your system? What people and personality traits feel safe to you? Are there political figures, symbols, or organizations that cue danger? Are there any that cue safety?

What songs or music genres do you dislike or avoid? What songs and music do you turn to that make you feel good?

Are there certain places that trigger danger or discomfort? What are the places that cue safety and a sense of relaxation?

Add any other reflections about your cues as you do this exercise. Practice awareness throughout the day and explore the cues your nervous system reads as dangerous or safe.

Scanning Neuroception

Learning to scan cues can help you tune into the unconscious process of neuroception. This exercise will teach you to scan the three environments neuroception is constantly reading and will take about ten minutes.

Get settled and find a quiet place to reflect. Take a few moments to center and focus on the present moment.

Begin by exploring **the environment around you**. *Slowly. Get curious and examine the space you're in.*

Notice everything you see: lighting, images, pictures, colors, objects, etc. Explore the space with curiosity and identify anything that suggests danger or safety.

Notice the smells around you. Then, notice the value your nervous system places on those smells.

Notice what you can hear and how your nervous system responds to that.

Notice what you can touch and feel. Notice the temperature, airflow, and any textures or sensations.

Get curious about everything you can see, smell, touch, and hear in your space, and notice how your nervous system automatically responds. As you practice this exercise, make any changes to your environment that feel appealing to you.

Shift your awareness now to your **physical body.** *As you reflect inward, you might close your eyes or find a place for your gaze to rest.*

Become aware of the physical sensations of your body.

Where do you feel tense, relaxed, loose, or tight?

What is your hunger level right now?

What discomfort or comfort do you notice in your body?

How's your energy today?

What's your temperature like?

Are you rested, or do you feel tired?

As you become aware of these bodily sensations, notice the value you automatically place on them. Notice what feels safe and comfortable and any sensations that feel dangerous or threatening to your system.

Make any changes that feel appealing to you as you practice scanning your internal environment.

Finally, if any **people or animals** *are around you, explore how neuroception is reading them. If you're alone, skip this step, but practice it next time you're around people or furry critters.*

> *How do these people or animals feel to your nervous system?*

> *Consider how eye contact, proximity, vocal tones, facial expressions, and physical gestures inform your experience with these creatures.*

> *What are the cues your system is appraising?*

What feels safe and comfortable, and what feels dangerous and potentially threatening?

You can practice this exercise throughout the day. The more you practice this, the quicker you'll be able to notice when your system is reading danger or safety. This is the art of turning a passive process into an active one and learning to apply polyvagal theory to your life. The better you get at identifying danger cues, the more empowered you are to respond and manage emotional reactions. Additionally, the better you can identify safety cues, the easier it becomes to calm down when you're feeling emotionally overwhelmed.

Where Attention Goes, Energy Flows

Sometimes, neuroception can cause an autonomic response that's bigger than necessary. After all, work deadlines can be stressful. But do they really warrant a panic attack? Probably not. While you might logically know this, your autonomic nervous system might have missed the memo. When neuroception is flooded with stress cues, our autonomic pathways can take us on a wild, chaotic, emotional ride. But you can hit the brake. When your autonomic nervous system moves into defensive pathways because of stressors, intentionally scanning for cues of comfort, safety, or peace can help you regain some control.

Not too long ago, I was traveling abroad to present at a conference. Getting to my destination ended up being a very stressful experience. Due to an unforeseen highway closure caused by a multi-car accident, followed by a storm, we missed a flight and had multiple connecting flights delayed. It was a mess. By the time we arrived at the last airport for our last connection, we had been traveling for two days. We were jet-lagged, exhausted, and in one of the busiest terminals in the world. It was a situation full of danger cues and opportunities for an emotional meltdown.

As we were waiting for our final flight, I noticed how overwhelmed and anxious I felt. My stress level was through the roof. My heart was racing, my shoulders were tense, and my breathing was shallow. My mind felt scattered, my jaw was locked, and I was hungry and not hungry all at the same time. These are my telltale markers that my autonomic nervous system is activated in sympathetic mobilization.

I noticed that I didn't have much connection to my ventral pathway, and my sympathetic nervous system was causing me to feel more stressed out than I needed to be. Neuroception was responding to an array of cues that it deemed to be stressful and dangerous, but the response was a complete overshoot. I didn't need all of those stress reactions at that moment. They weren't helping me. In fact, they were making everything worse. While travel is stressful, my level of autonomic response wasn't improving the situation, helping me get to my final destination any quicker, or allowing me to enjoy my experience. I wasn't in danger, there was no threat to my life, and nothing imminent was about to happen. Therefore, even though my nervous system was trying to be helpful with fight-or-flight energy, the response was way more than the situation required. I needed to cool my sympathetic system if I wanted to feel better.

Applying the knowledge of polyvagal theory and using my neuroception as a portal, I got curious. I actively started scanning the cues my system was reacting to, starting with my external environment. As I used my senses to scan my environment, I became aware of a barrage of stimuli that was getting my sympathetic pathway revved up in defensiveness. Bright lights, crowds of people, too many signs to read, not knowing where to go, and constant noise were big triggers for my system. Turning my awareness to my body, I noticed danger cues stemming from jet lag, feeling physically uncomfortable after sitting on a plane for way too long and needing a shower and a change of clothes. I then scanned the cues my system was reading in other people and noticed my system was hyperfocused on my husband's signals. My husband was also feeling exhausted and prickly. Understandably so. He was making less eye contact with me, his jaw was tight, and he was cranky. His cues of overwhelm fueled my already elevated nervous system as my neuroception read his stress signals. I was getting more stressed because he was stressed!

"Where attention goes, energy flows," I thought. My neuroception had its attention locked on all of the cues that it read to be dangerous, and my autonomic nervous system was coming along for the ride. So, I shifted my attention to look for safety cues. I knew my sympathetic response would lessen if I could increase awareness of safety, comfort, and calm. I put on my noise-canceling headphones to drown out what I found to be overstimulating sounds. I did not put on my headphones to listen to music because more noise would have added to my stress level. I used my headphones to reduce the cacophony of sound that was flooding my ears. "That's better," I thought.

Next, I took a few drinks of water, slowly feeling the cold sensation in the back of my throat. That felt good and gave me the idea to try a breath mint. I popped a mint in my mouth and focused on the taste and the sensation of the candy. Continuing to increase safety cues for my body, I stood up and stretched, releasing some tension. I walked over to a corner to do some simple yoga postures…a forward fold, a standing side stretch, and a hip flexor stretch helped my body relax, which in turn sent safety cues to neuroception. I started paying attention to my breath and took long, slow inhales and exhales. This was also a way to cue safety to my system. I was back in my body and feeling a little more regulated.

Next, I scanned the environment for a visual cue of safety, found the blue sky out the window, and rested my awareness there for about a minute. Finally, I turned to my husband, gave him a hug, and told him I loved him. He smiled and hugged me back. His smile, his hug, and his words were cues of safety. In about five minutes, I shifted my neuroception to taking in cues of safety over cues of danger. I was able to get closer to feeling emotionally regulated. Did that mean I was suddenly zenned out as if I had just walked out of a spa day? No. I was still in a very busy airport, jet-lagged, and had another flight to get through. But did my level of overwhelm significantly reduce to a tolerable level? It sure did.

When you notice your nervous system getting swept away with an unnecessary defensive response, you can use the knowledge of how your system works to turn things around. If your system is only paying attention to cues of danger or stress, your autonomic pathways will follow suit. But if you shift your attention to cues that feel safe or comforting, you can change the energy in your body. Where neuroception's attention goes, autonomic energy flows. By intentionally looking for cues of safety in the environment around us, inside our body, and with those we're in contact with, we can shift our attention and awareness away from danger toward safety. We can become active participants in the experience rather than passive bystanders. Although neuroception happens automatically, we can use our conscious brains to influence our biology by intentionally shifting what our systems are focusing on. By redirecting our attention, we can redirect our autonomic nervous systems and calm our stress responses.

Increasing Cues of Safety

To shift your autonomic state, you can focus on cues that your system perceives to be safe, comforting, or peaceful. This is how you can redirect the attention of your neuroception, moving it away from focusing on danger and stress and, in doing so, reduce autonomic overwhelm.

Scan each of the three domains that neuroception reads: the environment, your body, and people or animals around you. Intentionally look for stimuli or cues that feel appealing and calming. Focus on the cues that your system deems to be "safe."

Work with your five senses as you scan environmental cues. You might reduce your exposure to a cue of danger, such as putting on headphones to dampen the sound or resting your gaze on a picture that you like. You can choose to either change your exposure to a cue of danger or intentionally engage in a cue of safety.

Next, scan your body for cues of danger and safety and actively increase your safety cues. You can do this through movement, breath, food, hydration, or stretching, to name a few.

Finally, scan the space in between you and other creatures. Whether that be animals or people, try to increase your cues of safety. You might move to another side of the room if you're sitting next to someone who's sending you lots of unpleasant cues, give your cat a quick snuggle, or text a loved one.

Here are some examples of my go-tos when I'm trying to increase cues of safety:

In my environment

- Take a whiff of lavender essential oil

- Rest my gaze out the window on trees, birds, or the sky

- Focus on the temperature in the room

- Rest my awareness on an exit or door

- Put on chill music or noise-canceling headphones to reduce environmental noise

My body

- Take slow, deep breaths

- Stand up and stretch

- Go for a walk

- Scan my body for a place that feels pleasant or neutral and rest my attention there

- Take a bath or a shower

People and animals

- Play with my dogs

- Snuggle my cats

- Smile at a stranger

- Hug my husband

- Call a friend

- Connect to my inner voice of compassion and wisdom

RESET

When you learn the power of neuroception, you gain invaluable strategies to work with your nervous system. Your conscious brain is a highly intelligent organ. You can use it to influence your automatic responses and refocus neuroception's attention. Remember, neuroception is an unconscious, passive, reactive process. It constantly scans for danger and threat and will react without logical, rational input. But that doesn't mean you are powerless over this unconscious process.

On the contrary, you can turn this unconscious process into an incredible coping strategy. One additional way you can work with neuroception and use it to decrease overwhelm is with a strategy I call RESET. RESET is a skill I use to shift my emotional state when I'm feeling overwhelmed using the power of neuroception.

RESET stands for *recognize, evaluate, scan, engage,* and *time.* Each step is a way to regain some control over an out-of-control autonomic process by using neuroception. Note the slower you go through this, the better. Moving slowly through each of these steps is a way to calm your nervous system. If you rush through these too quickly, they won't have an effect.

Recognize: Recognize what's happening by naming the experience. The way you recognize is to simply name the experience. "I am full-blown fight-or-flight energy right now," or "My dorsal pathway is making me shutdown" are examples. Recognize the experience by calling it what it is. Without recognition of the experience, there's not much you can do to intervene. Awareness is key. Using the awareness of your autonomic blueprint, identify when you're moving toward sympathetic mobilization or dorsal shutdown because of stress and perceived danger. Recognizing you're swept away in a defensive, autonomic response is the precursor to being able to do anything about it.

Evaluate: Evaluate your response. Is it needed and necessary? Is that pile of laundry truly a life threat? Does the disagreement with your spouse require this response? Is this response needed right now? Is this response helpful right now? If the answer is yes, then recognize those responses are serving a purpose. If the response is no, move on to the following steps to get some control back.

Scan: Scan for cues of danger, identifying the cues your nervous system is responding to. What are the environmental, bodily, and interpersonal cues your system is reacting to? Use the scanning neuroception exercise from this chapter to identify the danger cues you're reacting to. Notice all of the stimuli that neuroception is reading and responding to.

Engage: Engage with safety cues. Look for external cues, bodily cues, and interpersonal cues that shift your awareness away from threats toward cues of safety. Become active in the experience and help your nervous system shift its attention. Remember, where attention goes, energy flows! Scan for cues that feel safe, pleasant, and calming, and allow yourself to connect to those cues.

Time: Time to turn it around. Those defensive survival responses get activated in a split second. But they take time to dissipate and calm. Dampening those stress responses doesn't happen in the blink of an eye. How much time you need to spend focusing on those safety cues is very much based on how big the stressor and stress responses are and how jumpy your system is. And, the more you practice these skills, the easier it gets over time to calm the inner storm.

Highlights and Takeaways

- The human body's autonomic nervous system is a powerful defender that prioritizes survival above all else. It detects, predicts, and responds to threats without conscious awareness through a process called neuroception.

- Neuroception scans three environments for cues of safety or danger. These three environments include the external environment, the physical body, and the people or animals you're in contact with.

- Neuroception is like a personal home surveillance system, always on and scanning for threats without input from the conscious parts of your brain. It activates autonomic defenses when it detects a threat, something unpleasant, or something stressful.

- Danger cues may be imminent threats, but they can also be understood as stimuli your system deems unpleasant, stressful, or threatening.

- Safety cues are stimuli your system finds calming, comforting, and soothing.

- Everyone has unique cues of danger and safety. Becoming aware of your cues and learning how your nervous system appraises information it comes into contact with can help you make the passive process of neuroception an active one.

- Where attention goes, energy flows. If left unchecked, neuroception can become overly focused on cues of danger that may not actually be dangerous. This can lead to emotional overwhelm and feeling like your nervous system is running the show.

- You can learn to turn the passive process of neuroception into an active one with polyvagal-informed skills. This includes learning to identify your cues of danger and safety, increasing your awareness of safety cues, and practicing the RESET technique.

Chapter 5

Vagal Tone

Did you know that you can exercise and tone your vagus nerve? Strengthening this part of your nervous system can give you greater control over your automatic defenses that arise in response to stress and danger. Just as you can shape and tone your muscles with exercise, you can do the same for your vagus nerve. Metaphorically speaking. Using techniques that tone the vagus nerve can enhance your neurological fitness and improve your ability to handle stress.

In this chapter, we will explore the concept of *vagal tone* and its influence on psychological and physical well-being. By understanding how the vagus nerve interacts with the body's autonomic pathways, you'll gain insight into the benefits of vagal health. Furthermore, we will examine the relationship between the vagus nerve and the heart, revealing how these two systems interact with stress responses, emotional wellness, and resiliency.

Consider this: if you had a goal to lift 100 pounds, you would probably focus on training and exercise to turn that goal into a reality. If you're already in good physical shape and you exercise regularly, you might be close to achieving this goal. If exercise and physical fitness are things you rarely engage in, you may be facing a longer journey to reach that 100-pound goal. Just as physical fitness directly correlates to your ability to lift 100 pounds in weight, neurophysiological fitness directly correlates to how well you manage stress. Through targeted vagal exercises, you can fortify your nervous system and become more resilient.

In this chapter, you will uncover the power of *vagal flexibility* and learn how it's influenced by the *vagal brake*. You'll get to assess how toned your vagus nerve is and build a framework for getting your vagus nerve to the gym (metaphorically speaking). To begin this journey, we must first examine the vital relationship between the vagus and the heart. So, let's dive in by learning about the relationship between your ticker and your vagus nerve.

The Heart of the Matter

Your vagus nerve and your heart are intimately connected. The functioning of one influences the functioning of the other. That's partly because your vagus nerve functions as an internal pacemaker. It is one of several mechanisms that make your heartbeat. Because of this connection, your heart rate influences your autonomic pathways. As heart rate increases and decreases, so does energy in autonomic pathways. These changes to heart rate and autonomic pathways influence your breathing, digestion, blood flow, thoughts, feelings, sensations, and even behaviors. The relationship between the vagus nerve and your heart is therefore uber important for understanding stress and emotional wellness. While you probably don't think about your heart much when you think of stress, this organ has huge implications for health and happiness.

Did you know that an ideal heart rate increases and decreases throughout the day? That's right. Your heart shouldn't beat like a metronome. Sometimes, you need your heart to beat fast; sometimes, you need it to beat slow. When you wake up, go for a walk, have intimate moments, or present in front of an audience, your vagus nerve ideally kicks your heart rate up a bit so you have energy to perform. When you sleep, snuggle with a pet or loved one, chill out to a movie, or meditate, a slower heart rate allows you to participate fully in these activities. A fast heart rate mobilizes and engages the sympathetic pathway, allowing you to experience motivation and energizing states. A regular heart rate varies in response to how your nervous system influences your heart's pacemaker. The ventral pathway helps create rhythmic variations in heartrate, allowing you to feel calm and at peace. A super slow heart rate can engage the immobilizing properties of the dorsal pathway, which may leave you feeling slow and sluggish. However, it's important to note that even those with outstanding cardio fitness, like professional athletes, can have a low resting heart rate.

Heart rate variability is a term that describes how much heartbeats fluctuate throughout the day. *Low heart rate variability* means that the heart beats like a metronome, likely too slow or too fast. A heart rate that is always too slow or too fast can be incredibly uncomfortable and problematic. Conversely, *high heart rate variability* means that heartbeats increase and decrease throughout the day in response to your dynamic nervous system. In general, higher heart rate variability is associated with enhanced vagal functioning. Thus, high heart rate variability is therefore associated with enhanced abilities to regulate and manage emotions along with less worry, stress, and rumination (Mather and Thayer 2018).

Because we need our heart rates to change in response to life demands and activities, an ideal heart rate changes throughout the day in response to environmental stimuli and what you're doing (e.g., having a snack on the couch or gearing up to run a marathon). If it doesn't, we get stuck in autonomic states of sympathetic overwhelm or dorsal shutdown. Sleep, concentration, and feeling peaceful are hard or impossible if the heart regularly beats too fast. Likewise, if the heart regularly beats too slowly, getting out of bed and finding the motivation to get through the day is a significant challenge. A healthy heart doesn't keep a steady rhythm...it keeps a variable rhythm. This is heart rate variability: fluctuations in heart rhythms that align with environmental stimuli and life demands.

Consider what your heart rate is like when you feel anxious. In anxiety and panic states, the heart beats fast. That racing heart cues your sympathetic pathway to mobilize, contributing to symptoms of anxiety and panic, racing thoughts, and restlessness. Coping skills for managing anxiety, such as grounding and breathing exercises (which we will review in chapter 6), lower heart rate and demonstrate a protective function of the vagus nerve. This vagal state gives the sympathetic pathway a chill pill. Likewise, when you feel shut down in the dorsal pathway, your heart rate is likely moving at a sluggish rate, contributing to a lack of motivation, feeling tired, exhausted, and flatter than a pancake. Coping skills (also ahead in chapter 6) for moving out of dorsal shutdown can increase heart rate, giving you access to the energy you need to get through the day.

Your heart rate is influenced by multiple factors. Not all heart conditions are due to your vagus nerve or a lack of coping skills. There's an entourage of things that influence your heart, including biological, environmental, psychological, and socioeconomic factors. But when it comes to stress, the vagus is front and center stage with a leading role in how you respond to life's curveballs.

Tracking Heart Rate

Do you ever track your heart rate throughout the day? If you have a smartwatch or a fitness tracker, you probably do. If you haven't, it might be time to get one to better understand how your vagus and ticker interact.

According to Harvard Health, a healthy and normal resting heart rate for adults is 60–100 beats per minute (Olshansky et al. 2023). That rate should change depending on what you're doing and the stimuli you're engaged with. You can check your heart rate with a heart rate tracker or with the old-fashioned route, which involves counting your heartbeats for fifteen seconds and multiplying that by four.

For the next week, check your heart rate at least two to three times daily. This is a simple way to get curious about how your heart rate changes throughout the day and how it correlates to your mood, energy, health, and wellness. Do you notice that your heart rate changes during certain activities? Does it change with your mood? Does it change at various points of the day? You can develop a new relationship with your heart as you attune to these patterns and variances.

Here are some questions to ponder as you check your heart rate:

1. What am I doing? (e.g., waking up, working out, reading a book, walking, etc.)

2. How do I feel emotionally?

3. How do I feel physically?

4. How is my energy level?

You will likely find patterns and correlations between your heart rate and activities, mood, physical sensations, and energy levels. The more you check your heart rate and practice this exercise, the more data you will have to learn from.

If this exercise results in any concerns about your heart, see your doctor. Heart disease is a leading cause of death, and preventative care is the number one way to reduce risk.

Vagal Flexibility and the Vagal Brake

Vagal flexibility is a term that refers to the ability of the vagus nerve to "modulate vagal responses to fit a dynamic range of challenges" (Spangler and McGinley 2020). Ummm…what? In simpler terms, vagal flexibility refers to how well your vagus nerve can change your heart rate to meet the needs of your life. The more flexible your vagus nerve, the more likely it is that you have high heart rate variability.

To live your best life and feel your best while doing it, you need your heart to keep up with you. And for your heart to make life easier rather than harder, you need a flexible vagus nerve. It's that simple. Without this flexibility, we can get stuck in a rut. We might feel chronically overwhelmed, stressed out, anxious, depressed, and shut down without a way out. Vagal flexibility allows us to respond to life with emotional flexibility. We can bend, flex, and maneuver around life's upsets rather than becoming engulfed in autonomic stress responses.

When we encounter a stressor or a life-threatening situation, changes in heart rate help us navigate those moments and may even save our lives. But what if we get stuck in those states even when the stressor is over? Or what if we encounter an annoyance or stressor and our heart rate misses the mark by going to one extreme or the other (too slow or too fast), making the response more problematic than helpful. This inability to move out of activated autonomic pathways, getting hijacked by extremes, indicates that the vagus nerve needs some TLC and training. While those changes in energy can be helpful and lifesaving, they are not helpful if they surpass a threshold of tolerance or if we get trapped in those states when they aren't needed.

Stephen Porges coined the term "vagal brake" to refer to the mechanism that allows the vagus to increase and decrease heart rate (Porges 2011). When the vagal brake engages, heart rate decreases, and when the brake is removed, heart rate increases. Just like a brake on a car helps regulate speed, the vagal brake helps regulate the speed of the heart. When our vagal brake is flexible, we can regulate heart rate in response to circumstances, needs, events, and stressors. A flexible vagal brake is a very precious thing to have in life. It's a one-way ticket to having more health, wellness, and happiness.

Vagal flexibility is associated with several important health metrics (Spangler and McGinley 2020). It plays a role in cognitive inhibition control, which is the ability to use executive functions, such as logic and reasoning, to inhibit knee-jerk reactions. For example, when someone cuts you off on the highway, cognitive inhibition control allows you to inhibit the urge to scream, curse, or give the middle finger.

Vagal flexibility has also been linked to being less distracted by emotions. This means unpleasant emotions don't preoccupy you or take up all of your mental real estate. For example, say you have a difficult phone call with a family member that stirred up some old stuff and tender feelings. Rather than being consumed and distracted by those big emotions for the rest of the day, vagal flexibility can help you regulate, refocus, and move on.

Without vagal flexibility, stress is more likely to hijack your autonomic nervous system. You might feel like you're held hostage by your emotions. And when we feel like our emotions run the show, we tend to feel run over by life. You might feel like you're constantly running from invisible threats or utterly paralyzed and unable to make a decision or move. And let's be honest. When your emotions are calling the shots, life feels more like a monster truck rally than a smooth, leisurely ride.

While vagal flexibility doesn't mean you will never feel the mighty power of big emotions, it does make it possible to get back to a state of balance faster and with less disruption. We cannot change the fact that life is going to be stressful and hard. But there's a lot we can do to equip our nervous system with tools to cope. By developing a flexible vagal brake, you can improve your ability to influence heart rate, increase and decrease the energy of autonomic pathways, and become more resilient. You can achieve this by engaging in exercises that tone the vagus nerve.

Visualize Your Vagal Brake

Let's use the power of imagery to create a connection to your vagal brake. As you think about the vagal brake's ability to increase and decrease energy, think of an image that goes along with this concept. Personally, I envision my vagal brake as a dam that manages the flow of energy. When my vagal brake is engaged, the dam closes, which means less energy is flowing through my nervous system. The result is that things calm down inside.

Conversely, when the vagal brake is released, the dam opens, leading to an influx of energy, motivation, and mobilization. When the dam is wide open, my sympathetic nervous system is fully mobilized. I feel a flood of energy moving throughout my mind and body. When the dam is closed shut, I experience dorsal shutdown and feel a drought of energy throughout my mind and body.

What visual representation appeals to you as you think of the vagal brake and its impact on your autonomic pathways? This can be anything that represents these concepts for you. Some examples include dials on a stove, the volume buttons on a remote control, wind in the sails of a sailboat, or a dimmer switch. Get clear about the imagery that helps you relate to this concept.

Next, explore these reflection questions:

1. What's the current state of my vagal brake? What "setting" or level is it on (depending on your visual, use the wording that fits best).

2. Do I have too much, too little, or just enough energy?

3. How do I know? What information am I using to decipher the state of my vagal brake and my energy level? What do I notice in my autonomic pathways?

This practice will help you develop heightened self-awareness of your vagal brake and autonomic pathways. This valuable information allows you to interact with an otherwise automatic process in a way that supports your quality of life. Check in with your vagal brake imagery a few times a day, especially when you're feeling unpleasant feelings or sensations. Regular reflection allows you to create a new relationship with these concepts. Understanding your vagal brake and energy levels can unlock new possibilities for self-regulation and personal growth.

Exercising the Vagus Nerve

So, how do you get a flexible vagus nerve? Is it really possible to improve the functioning of my nervous system and, in doing so, feel less stressed out and emotionally overwhelmed? Yes. You absolutely can. You can accomplish this by engaging in activities that tone the vagus nerve through *vagal exercises*. Vagal exercises are like pull-ups and push-ups for your vagus nerve. They help you get toned from the inside out.

Building vagal tone doesn't happen by staying comfy, cushy, and stagnant on the couch. It requires you to "work out" or exercise your nervous system. To tone that vagus like a six-pack of abs, you have to practice exercises that engage and disengage the vagal brake. The more you exercise the brake, the more flexible and toned your vagus becomes. In chapter 6, I'll guide you through a number of vagal exercises with step-by-step instructions. But for now, let's explore this concept further and assess how toned your vagus nerve currently is.

Vagal exercises are skills that intentionally influence heart rate. Note that not everything that influences your heart rate is a vagal exercise. For example, drinking three shots of espresso to get over the afternoon slump will influence your heart rate, but it's not a vagal exercise. It's a way of using a substance to change the functioning of your neurophysiological state. However, strategies like yoga, exercise, and mindfulness are natural and adaptive ways to exercise and tone the vagus.

We've been using the metaphor of working out in this chapter, and in fact, exercise is a great way to tone your vagus nerve (Stanley et al. 2013)! Engaging in cardiovascular exercise or weightlifting will naturally increase your heart rate. If you're lifting weights, you lift for a certain number of reps, then rest for thirty to sixty seconds. As you lift weights, your heart rate increases, and as you rest, your heart rate decreases. The same goes for cardiovascular exercises. When you take a brisk walk, your heart rate increases, and when you stop to rest, your heart rate decreases. Whether you have the stamina to lift five-pound weights for five minutes or run several miles over five hours, your vagus nerve benefits from physical movement and exercise because of your heart.

How Toned Is My Vagus?

Has all this got you wondering how toned your vagus nerve is? Take this self-assessment and explore how flexible your nervous system is. This is not a diagnostic, scientific assessment. These questions are oriented toward symptoms and behaviors that are correlated with vagal functioning (Cabrera et al. 2018). The purpose of this assessment is to invite personal inquiry and deepen self-awareness.

Answer True or False for each question. Give yourself one point for every question you answer as True:

1. When I feel unpleasant emotions, it is hard for me to calm down.

2. I struggle to organize my thoughts and thinking. My mind feels jumbled and unclear.

3. I have a hard time finding the energy I need to get through ·the day.

4. I have a hard time calming down when I need to sit still or rest. I have too much energy in my body.

5. I rarely feel peaceful and calm.

6. I struggle with depression, anxiety, panic, rage, fear, anger, or feeling overwhelmed.

7. I have a hard time connecting with others.

8. It's hard for me to trust people.

9. I can't identify many good things about myself.

10. I struggle to cope and regulate my emotions.

11. I struggle to get restful sleep. That may include difficulties getting to sleep, difficulties sleeping through the night, night terrors, sleepwalking, or sleep apnea.

12. It's hard to focus and pay attention.

13. I have frequent digestive problems. This may include nausea, gas, bloating, acid reflux, digestive issues, abdominal pain, and increased or decreased appetite.

14. I struggle to think about the future and set goals.

15. I often feel stuck in unpleasant feelings and sensations in my mind and body.

Add up how many True responses you had and find your score below.

A score of 0–5 is indicative of a well-regulated nervous system with high vagal tone and a flexible vagus. Having a flexible vagus nerve allows your mind and body to regulate and gives you access to more health and wellness.

A score of 6–9 may indicate that you have moderate levels regulation and vagal tone. While your vagus nerve has some flexibility, you still get stuck in autonomic states that can lead to emotional and physical suffering.

A score of 10+ may indicate a poorly regulated autonomic system with low vagal tone and limited vagal flexibility. You may struggle to regulate emotions, often feel uncomfortable physical sensations, and have significant sleep problems and poor digestion. Low vagal tone means that your vagus nerve is not able to optimally function in a manner that supports your health and wellness. This can lead to considerable amounts of emotional and physical suffering.

Finding Middle Ground

No matter where you fall on the self-assessment scale, your nervous system is capable of becoming more resilient. It has the remarkable ability to heal and form new neural pathways. This means that you have the potential to nurture and exercise your vagus nerve, boosting its functionality and improving its ability to regulate autonomic pathways.

Certain medical and psychological conditions such as heart conditions, autism, and traumatic brain injury may not respond solely to skill-based interventions. It's important to take these conditions seriously as they can profoundly impact vagal functioning. This chapter does not aim to suggest that everything can be solved through self-help strategies or that every condition can be fixed through vagal exercises. The nervous system is complex, and many factors affect its functioning. Some of those things are in your control, and some aren't. But even if you have a diagnosis or condition that affects your vagus nerve, skills and strategies can still make a positive change. Do not assume that everything in this book will work for you. Likewise, don't assume that nothing in this book will work because of a condition or diagnosis. Find the middle ground and embark on this polyvagal journey with a curious mind.

Using the Vagal Brake

A few years ago, I was out on a hike with my husband and our dog in the Rocky Mountains when we got caught up in an unexpected rainstorm. That storm quickly turned into a serious threat as it started hailing, and water was rushing through the gully, posing a threat of a flash flood. There was lightning overhead, and the downpour of cold water at 9,000 feet posed an additional threat of hypothermia.

We found a rock to crouch under and tried to hunker down there, the two of us and our dog, and wait it out. We quickly realized that we were in some real trouble. There was water pouring down from over the rock, and I was afraid of a flash flood or a mudslide. After thirty minutes in this storm, we were freezing, and I noticed my husband was starting to show some signs of hypothermia as his lips were turning blue. There was so much hail and rain we couldn't see the trail and therefore couldn't escape.

This was a moment when my autonomic pathways started to take over, and I felt myself moving into fight or flight. As I had been studying polyvagal theory and was able to notice my telltale signs of sympathetic, I used some skills to engage my vagal brake. I knew that maintaining a connection to my ventral pathway would help me navigate this tricky and dangerous situation. I used a breathing technique I learned in yoga (see Abdominal Breathing in chapter 6) that generates core body heat and helps me stay tethered to my ventral circuit. By using this breathing technique I was able to warm up my core and engage my vagal brake. Engaging my vagal brake allowed me to think more clearly, an invaluable survival tool at that moment. My husband wanted to make a run for it. But as we couldn't see the trail, we weren't sure which way we were going, and we'd be running into the danger zone if a flash flood or mudslide came barreling through. That fight-or-flight response might not be the best chance for our survival. I showed him how to breathe the way I was doing and encouraged him to wait just a little longer. The Rocky Mountains are notorious for torrential downpours that quickly pass through.

We waited a few more minutes, and sure enough, the rain let up. As soon as we could see the trail, we made a break.

My husband, at this point, was looking pretty rough. While he's an avid outdoorsman, he tried to shield our dog and me from the downpour, which meant he had been more exposed to the cold rain than I had been. He was pale and his lips were blue. He was talking a little nonsensically, and he said he couldn't feel his hands or feet. I led the way and encouraged him to open and close his hands, to move quickly down the trail and get his blood flowing. Because I was connected to my ventral pathway, I was able to coregulate him by coaching him to breathe, keep moving, and constantly wiggle his fingers and toes to get blood flowing.

The car was about a mile away, and in no time, we made it back, grabbed some towels, and looked up to find a clear blue sky mocking us. Our dog was fine too, just a little shaken from the whole ordeal. We took off our wet clothes, blasted the heat, drank a bunch of water, and looked at each other in shock and amazement.

Our nervous systems were responding to some very clear cues of danger in that situation. The fight-or-flight energy we were feeling from the activation of our sympathetic pathways was very much needed and warranted. But, if we had impulsively reacted to those fight-or-flight urges, I'm not sure things would have ended as well. Because we used breath to engage our vagal brakes and create some much-needed body heat, we were able to think through the situation with a bit more clarity. We were able to dampen our impulses and make thoughtful decisions. Using our vagal brakes allowed us to use cognitive inhibition and reasoning to make decisions, getting us back to the car drenched but free of injury.

Having skills to work your vagal brake is to your benefit. Being able to engage the brake and give your autonomic and automatic survival responses a chill pill can be really helpful in a life-or-death situation, a heated argument, or a highly stressful situation that needs thoughtful problem-solving. When we can use skills to increase our connection with the ventral pathway, moving away from extreme states of fight, flight, freeze, or collapse, we often find ourselves with more options, choices, and resources to navigate the situation. The ability to engage your vagal brake is a must when it comes to developing effective tools to cope with stress, working through adversity, and finding emotional balance. In the next chapters, we'll dive into strategies that help you engage your vagal brake, build vagal tone, and maintain that oh-so-precious connection with ventral in even the most stressful situations.

Highlights and Takeaways

- It is possible to exercise and tone the vagus nerve similar to how you can tone your muscles by working out.

- Toning the vagus nerve can improve neurological fitness, stress tolerance, and nervous system regulation.

- Heart rate variability describes fluctuations in heartbeats according to life demands. It is associated with better emotion regulation, impulse inhibition, and less anxiety.

- Vagal flexibility is essential for health and well-being.

- The vagal brake is the mechanism that enables the vagus nerve to influence heart rate.

- The vagus nerve can be toned by engaging in exercises (i.e., activities, behaviors, or skills) that increase and decrease heart rate.

- There are many ways to tone the vagus nerve. We will explore several in the next chapter. Techniques supported by research include but are not limited to cardiovascular exercise, weight-lifting, yoga, meditation, breath work, mindfulness, massage, prayer, therapy, cold water therapy, use of supplements, and connecting with a pet or loved one.

- These exercises can be adapted for anyone regardless of physical or neurological conditions.

Chapter 6

Vagal Exercises

As we've reviewed, a "toned" vagus nerve is a very good thing. A toned vagus nerve is a flexible vagus nerve. That means you can move in and out of autonomic pathways with greater ease, giving you more control over your feelings, bodily sensations, and thoughts. A flexible vagus nerve truly is an invaluable asset on this journey called life. It allows you to hit the brakes on anxiety and panic, get yourself out of a funk when you're feeling down and out, and manage stress responses like a pro as you deal with the big and little challenges of life. If you don't have a flexible vagus nerve, you might feel out of control over your emotions. It's easy to get stuck in states of overwhelm or shut down...which makes life hard and sucky.

So, if you want to feel more emotionally balanced, more regulated, more resilient, and less burdened by stress, you have to get to exercising your vagus nerve. You can't just will or think your vagus nerve into being more toned and flexible. You have to "work out" that vagal brake on a regular basis. The more you exercise the vagal brake, the more resilient you will be and better capable of bouncing back in the face of stress.

You can use a variety of strategies to tone your vagus nerve. Returning to the information outlined in chapter 2, remember that it all starts with a few foundational health habits. Sleep, nutrition, hydration, and socialization. While those four factors alone don't fix everything or create vagal tone in and of themselves, prioritizing them can lead to considerable shifts in well-being. If those four pillars aren't being prioritized, no amount of coping strategies, self-help books, or "hacks" will have an effect.

There is no way to get every activity that can tone your vagus nerve onto one list. Just like there are multiple ways to exercise your body, there are many, many ways to exercise your vagus nerve. So you can understand how broad the list could be, here are a few activities shown to help build a flexible vagus nerve (Laborde et al. 2018):

- Brain stimulation with transcranial magnetic stimulation

- Oxygen inhalation

- Supplements: omega-3, B12, vitamin D, and magnesium may impact heart rate variability

- Cold water immersion

- Cryotherapy

- Acupuncture

- Massage

- Meditation and mindfulness

- Qigong

- Reiki

- Theta frequency binaural beats

- Breathing exercises

- Yoga

- Prayer

- Calming music

- Singing

- Regular contact with other humans or animals

- Walking in nature

That's quite a list! As you can see, there are a lot of different activities and practices you can use to exercise the vagus nerve. You probably engage in a lot of these items on some level already. But the key now is to engage with these practices intentionally. Learning to recognize your autonomic pathways opens the doorway to work with your nervous system intentionally. When you understand which techniques affect your vagus, you can engage with the right skill at the right time.

For example, maybe you choose to take a walk at lunch to exercise your vagal brake, and you intentionally choose a route that's full of cues of safety for you. You walk down a street with some big, beautiful trees and take in a moment with nature. On your commute home, you, intentionally, choose to play some calming binaural beats and cook a meal that's high in omega-3s. Why? Because you know those are things that feed your neurobiology. You follow that up with a feel-good show on the couch with your cat, who is truly the cutest cat there ever was. You close up shop with a gratitude prayer, reflecting on your hopes for the future and all that you're grateful for, and you get to bed early to ensure you get plenty of sleep. That is a five-star vagus nerve kind of day.

With this knowledge comes the opportunity, and arguably, responsibility, to live your life with the needs of your nervous system at the forefront of your mind. No one is responsible for your neurons but you. You are the caretaker of your neurobiology. And when you take good care of your nervous system, it is better equipped to take good care of you.

Somatic Techniques

Somatic techniques connect the mind and body to release tension, promote regulation, and support well-being. They often focus on physical exercises or mindfulness-based practices rather than using the cognitive, rational thinking brain to regulate. Somatic techniques are an incredible opportunity to work with the vagus nerve.

This section contains some of my favorite somatic skills for working with my autonomic pathways and engaging my vagus nerve. You too can use these techniques to train and tone your vagus nerve. You can also use these strategies to work with your vagal brake and decrease dorsal or sympathetic activation in moments of overwhelm. Techniques in this chapter are designed to tone the vagus and apply the vagal brake through body-based or somatic-focused interventions.

Yoga Nidra

Yoga is an internationally recognized practice and comes with a smorgasbord of health benefits. While many people in Western cultures think of yoga as a practice in which you put yourself into some pretzel-like pose, this is not an accurate representation of yoga. Yoga, as a word, can be roughly translated to "union." It is a practice that seeks to create a union between mind, body, heart, and spirit. There are many forms of yoga, multiple lineages, and a variety of traditions. Beyond the physical postures or poses, yoga is also practiced through reading, chanting, meditation, mindfulness, physical movement, and serving others. Studies indicate that certain yogic practices can positively affect heart rate variability and vagal tone (Bandi Krishna et al. 2014; Ferreira-Vorkapic et al. 2018; Markil et al. 2012; Rajagopalan et al. 2022). This means that yoga comes with a host of benefits and ways to work out your vagus.

Yoga nidra is a meditative, therapeutic form of yoga. It is on my personal list of the top three best self-help strategies of all time. "Nidra" is a Sanskrit word that roughly translates to "sleep" because nidra is the practice of "yogic sleep." Yoga nidra does not require physical postures or balancing acts. It is best practiced lying down with cozy blankets and pillows. Yoga nidra involves progressive relaxation of the body followed by guided imagery. You can easily find yoga nidra recordings on the internet, and anywhere you stream music. Some recordings are ten minutes, and some are eight hours! If you're new to yoga nidra and enjoy this exercise, you have a wealth of free resources online available to you.

If you would prefer to listen to this exercise, you can find the link in chapter 2.

Yoga Nidra Progressive Relaxation Exercise

This exercise takes about fifteen minutes.

Get cozy. Lie down with some blankets and pillows. You might set a timer as there is a real risk of falling asleep when you practice yoga nidra.

Move through this practice slowly—the slower, the better. You can also visit the recorded version by following the audio link.

Once you're comfortable, bring your awareness to your breath. Notice your breath as it moves in and out of your lungs.

Notice the sensation of your breath in the back of your throat. Notice the temperature of your breath.

Notice the sensation in your lungs on the inhale and the exhale.

Bring your awareness to the crown of your head. Relax all the muscles in your scalp.

Relax the face, the eyes, the jaw, the throat.

Continue that awareness down the right arm, allowing it to get heavier at your side.

Take your awareness down your left arm and allow it to get heavier at your side.

Allow the upper back, middle, and lower back to relax.

Release any tension you're holding in your abdomen.

Allow your pelvis and hips to relax.

Take your awareness down your right leg very slowly, relaxing all of the muscles down your leg to your toes.

Now, take your awareness to your left leg and relax all of the muscles as you take your awareness down to your toes.

Become aware of your entire body again.

Notice your entire body is relaxed and breathing.

Notice the sensations in your body. What do you feel?

Notice where you sense energy pulsing, throbbing, flowing, fluttering, or radiating.

Notice places in your body where you feel more energy.

Notice places in your body where you feel less energy.

Refrain from judgment. There's no need to judge your nervous system.

Observe.

Notice.

Be curious.

Now, picture a healing light hovering just above you. This bright healing light is here to offer nurturing and support, freeing you of stress, worry, pain, and discomfort.

Picture yourself being wrapped up in this ball of healing light and energy.

Imagine it wrapping around you like a warm, cozy blanket. From your head to your toes, picture this energy enveloping you, nourishing you, and filling every inch of your body with peace.

With each breath, allow the light to embrace you even more.

As this healing light holds you, welcome in more peace and more ease.

Stay here, focused on the light, your breathing, and your feelings as long as they feel good.

When you're ready, come out of this practice very slowly.

Start by wiggling your fingers and toes. Stretch and find some very gentle movement.

Finally, open your eyes, roll onto one side, and then push yourself up to sit.

Pause here and reflect.

1.   *What feelings are you aware of at this moment?*

2.   *What bodily sensations are you aware of?*

3.   *Where are you on your autonomic blueprint?*

4.   *What reflections do you have about this practice?*

5.   *When are good times to turn to yoga nidra for support and regulation?*

Cold Water Therapy

Cold water, what? Yup! There's a thing called cold water therapy. It is quickly growing in popularity as a technique to improve mood and reduce symptoms of depression (Kelly and Bird 2022; Hjorth et al. 2022; Shevchuk et al. 2008). Cold water therapy involves direct exposure to cold water for brief periods. How "brief," you might ask? We're talking thirty seconds to twenty minutes for the advanced. Remember, though, hypothermia is a thing, and there is such a thing as too long when it comes to cold water therapy practice.

Cold water therapy stimulates and tones the vagus nerve. It is a wonderful vagal exercise because it influences your autonomic pathways. It has been demonstrated to improve mood and metabolism and reduce pain. One of the benefits is that cold water engages the vagal brake. That quick, instinctive gasp that happens when you get doused in cold water is your vagal brake engaging, causing your heart rate to quickly pick up. This knowledge helps my mental game when I practice cold water therapy. The moment that I gasp, I simply think, "This is the exercise! Vagal brake!"

There are several ways you can use cold water therapy:

- Splash your face with cold water

- Turn your shower to cold for the last 30–60 seconds

- Get a cold plunge

- Visit a cryogenic chamber

Always consult with your doctor first, especially if you have heart issues. The amount of time you immerse yourself will vary depending on your tolerance level and the form of cold water exposure. I recommend starting with the shower for ten seconds. Acclimate, then increase the time as you feel more comfortable.

When I first started practicing cold water therapy in the shower, I absolutely hated it. Every day I dreaded it and had to force myself to turn that knob to cold. I learned to psych myself up, chanting, "You can do this! It's just thirty seconds! That's less time than it takes to walk to the mailbox!" That voice has been really helpful in my practice. I also found that playing motivating music (whether in my head or on a speaker) was incredibly helpful. I kept pushing myself to do it every day. And now? Now, I crave my cold water time. Today, my showers typically involve a few cycles of cold water therapy, which involves fluctuating between cold and hot. When I'm sick or going through stressful times, I take multiple showers a day to get the cold water exposure and engage my vagal brake. I share this to be a cheerleader and emphasize that, yes, it gets better. Think of this story when you're cursing me in your shower and say, "One day, I'll crave this."

Breathwork

The vagal brake is directly connected to the breath. When you inhale, your vagal brake releases, causing your heart rate to increase. When you exhale, the vagal brake is applied, causing your heart rate to slow. Because your heart rate naturally increases and decreases as you breathe, breathwork is a sure strategy to interact with your vagal brake and build vagal flexibility. It is well documented that breathwork is a fabulous way to manage stress and improve well-being. One 2023 study by Balban and colleagues even claims that certain forms of breathwork are more effective in "improving mood and physiological arousal" than mindfulness or meditation training.

Research indicates that slow-paced breathing can influence autonomic pathways and heart rate variability. It has the potential to increase vagal tone (Laborde et al. 2017; Laborde et al. 2022), reduce anxiety (Magnon et al. 2021), and improve well-being (Goldstein et al. 2016). The following exercises will take you through a series of breathing practices that use slow-paced breathing to engage the vagal brake and develop vagal flexibility.

Bee Breath

The vagus nerve innervates, or touches, many places in the body. The larynx, which includes your vocal cords, is one of those locations. Practicing bee breath stimulates the vagus nerve via the vocal cords, and the long, slow exhale in this practice further engages the vagal brake. To practice bee breath, simply hum, like a bee buzzes, as you exhale.

Find a comfortable seat.

Take a cleansing inhale, then exhale.

Now, take a long inhale through your nose, filling the lungs with air.

With the mouth closed, hum as you exhale the air from your lungs. Try to make the exhale as long as you can.

Take another inhale.

Exhale again with the mouth closed, and hum or buzz like a bee.

Repeat for six or more rounds.

After your last exhale, allow your breath to return to normal. Notice what you feel inside. Become aware of any shifts in how your body feels, what's happening in your mind, and your emotional state.

Physiological Sigh

The *physiological sigh* is a simple breathing technique that can reduce anxiety and stress. It engages the vagal brake and, in doing so, reduces sympathetic activation. Research indicates that the physiological sigh can be a quick and easy way to change your neurophysiological state (Balban et al. 2023). This breathing exercise requires you to take *two* inhales followed by a long sigh with your mouth open. Let's practice.

Find a comfortable seat.

To begin, take a cleansing inhale through the nose and exhale through the mouth.

Now, take one long inhale through your nose, followed by an additional quick inhale through the nose.

Next, open your mouth and sigh, exhaling with your mouth open. Be sure to actually sigh, or it won't have the same effect!

Repeat this sequence by taking a long inhale through the nose, followed by one more quick inhale through the nose. Next, open your mouth and sigh as you exhale.

Practice this six times or for a few minutes.

Allow your breath to return to normal, and notice the sensations and feelings you're aware of. What do you notice inside? What's different?

Box Breathing

Box breathing is a technique you can practice virtually anywhere. Boxed breathing includes repetitions of inhaling, holding the breath at the top of the inhale, exhaling, and holding the breath at the bottom of the exhale. It focuses your mind as it creates an equal rhythm of the breath, leaving you feeling balanced and regulated.

Box breathing gets its name from the box that you draw as you practice this exercise. You can draw a box on paper, trace one in the air, or just picture a box in your mind, such as the one illustrated here. This is one way to keep your attention focused and prevent your mind from wandering.

Find a comfortable seat.

As you inhale, draw the top line of the box from left to right.

Hold at the top of the inhale and trace the side of the box from top to bottom.

Now exhale as you trace the bottom line of the box from right to left.

Finally, hold at the bottom of the exhale as you trace the last side of the box from the top to the bottom.

Repeat the whole sequence a few times or for a few minutes. And remember, the slower you go, the better.

Each time you repeat the sequence, slow the practice a little more.

After six or more rounds, let your breath return to normal and notice your experience. Become aware of any changes in your emotions, body sensations, and autonomic pathways.

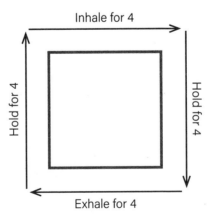

Inhale for 4

Hold for 4

Hold for 4

Exhale for 4

Bellows Breath

This is a technique I learned from my yoga teacher, Michael Shankara, in Denver, Colorado. It is a breathing technique that can increase sympathetic energy and help you move out of a state of dorsal shutdown. I use this technique to generate core body heat and get energized when I'm feeling flat. It requires you to focus on fully expanding and deflating your abdomen as you breathe. Because this exercise engages the abdomen and keeps your breath moving quickly, it can increase your heart rate along with core body temperature and sympathetic energy.

Find a comfortable seat.

Bring your awareness to your belly.

Take a quick, big inhale, and as you do, feel your belly fully expand.

Now exhale quickly and pull your belly toward your spine. This helps to expel all of the air from the lungs.

Keep this repetition going, and keep your focus on moving your belly as you breathe.

Do not pause at the top or bottom of the inhale. Rather, keep this cycle moving at a fast pace, engaging your abdominal muscles to fully extend and contract.

Practice for 30–60 seconds.

Check in and notice any changes in your body, emotions, or thoughts.

Mindfulness and Meditation

Research indicates potential improvements in vagal tone following mindfulness and meditation practices (Linares et al. 2019; Poli et al. 2021). However, meditation doesn't produce a calming effect for everyone every time. Some people feel more activated or worked up when they try to meditate. Let's consider some possible explanations for that.

As meditation requires one to sit still and turn inward, it can unpleasantly activate autonomic pathways if sitting still and turning inward is an uncomfortable experience.

As someone who has practiced meditation for many years, sometimes, if I sit down to meditate when feeling revved up in sympathetic overwhelm, I end up feeling more anxious. However, there have been many more times when meditation has positively affected me. Meditation can be a life-changing practice for many. But it's not necessarily easy and can sometimes leave us feeling worse. It depends on the state of our neurobiology and whether neuroception perceives sitting still, being quiet, and turning inward to be a safe or dangerous experience.

Meditation is a form of mindfulness. But not all mindfulness is meditation. For many, mindfulness can be a more approachable alternative to meditation, and it may even be the thing that teaches you the skills you need to meditate. Mindfulness-based strategies can positively affect vagal tone and increase activation of the ventral circuit (Poli et al. 2021). The following exercises are mindfulness techniques that can help to build vagal tone and a more flexible vagus nerve.

Heart-Focused Practice

This practice is inspired by *metta meditation*. I first practiced this exercise with the internationally known Buddhist monk and author Thich Nhat Hahn, who passed away in 2022. Metta is a school of mindfulness and contemplative practice that focuses on compassion. Practicing metta meditations can help you develop compassion for yourself and others. It involves slow breathing and focusing on your internal experience. This exercise may take five to ten minutes depending on how long you wish to practice. If you would prefer to listen, you can find the link in chapter 2.

To begin, find a comfortable seat. You might even choose to lie down.

Take a few slow breaths to settle in and find stillness.

Close your eyes or allow your gaze to rest.

Bring your awareness to your heart.

Bring one or both hands to rest over your heart.

Notice your heart beating.

Sit in this way for several moments or minutes, noticing your breath flow in and out along with the beating of your heart.

Next, add a simple mantra to keep your mind focused. On the inhale, say in your mind, "I am aware of my heart," and on the exhale, say, "May I have peace in my heart." You can slightly modify these phrases if there's a phrase that calls to you but try to keep them focused on your heart and holding compassion.

Sit for a few minutes, noticing your breath and your heart as you repeat the mantra "I am aware of my heart" and "may I have peace in my heart."

This heart-focused meta practice is a wonderful go-to when you're feeling hurt, lost, or out of sorts. Focusing on compassion for yourself and others can soothe activated autonomic pathways and increase your connection to the ventral.

A Ventral Anchor

Many contemplative practices include guided visualization. From mindfulness to meditation to yoga nidra, the power of the mind can be used to calm the nervous system and elicit desired states made possible by the ventral pathway. This exercise uses guided imagery to help you connect to your ventral pathway.

Find a comfortable place to sit or lie down.

Take a few slow breaths and settle into stillness.

Close your eyes or allow your gaze to rest.

Bring to mind all of the qualities of your ventral pathway. Use your word for ventral to call it into mind.

Connect with the restorative, peaceful, nourishing qualities of ventral.

Consider your thoughts, feelings, and behaviors when you're connected to this pathway.

Think of an image that best represents this pathway. It can be anything at all that fits. It might be a specific object, an animal, a spiritual symbol, a color, or a person.

Allow that image to expand in your mind. Notice the colors, shapes, and qualities that go along with this image.

As you hold this image in your mind, notice your feelings and sensations that come to life.

Can you feel your ventral pathway as you connect to this image? If you cannot, change the image until you find one that allows you to feel that connection.

Spend a few minutes holding this image in your mind while also noticing what you feel and sense in the body. Allow your connection to ventral to grow and expand.

When you're ready, slowly shift your attention away from the exercise. You might find some subtle movement or even stretch before opening your eyes.

Take a moment to reflect on your experience and what you are aware of after this practice.

You can use your ventral anchor to help you get back to this chill, peaceful pathway when you're feeling the grips of sympathetic or dorsal defenses. Use the image as an anchor or a way to tether to your ventral path. Simply call the image to mind when you need it and search for the feelings and sensations that accompany your ventral anchor in your body.

Nature

Spending time in nature is like a spa day for your vagus nerve. Whether you're taking a hike or just admiring a beautiful landscape, the natural world can be magic for the autonomic nervous system. Research supports that spending time in nature promotes peace and calm by reducing stress hormones and lowering blood pressure (Gladwell et al. 2012; Lee et al. 2014; Wells and Evans 2003).

How much time should you spend in nature each week? The good news is that you don't need to hike ten miles a week to reap these benefits. Experts suggest aiming for two hours a week.

The Five Senses

Next time you venture outdoors, take your five senses with you and deepen your connection to the natural world. You can do this while on a walk, a hike, or even just sitting in a park or any natural environment. Sift through your five senses and allow neuroception to take in all of the safety cues that nature has to offer.

Sight: Scan your surroundings and take in the natural environment. Engage your neuroceptive abilities by looking for cues that feel pleasant, appealing, and safe. Notice the light, the colors, and any natural objects. Allow your awareness to rest on those cues that feel pleasant, allowing your system to take them in. You may notice the light shining through the leaves, beautiful puffy clouds, or gorgeous colors made possible by a sunset. Slow down and savor those cues using the sense of sight.

Sound: Notice the sound cues that feel safe and appealing. I like to close my eyes as I do this as it allows my sense of sound to focus even more fully on certain tones and noises that feel good to my nervous system. Allow your awareness to rest on the quiet around you, the sound of water, or the wind in the trees. If you're in a public place or urban environment, perhaps you hear children laughing, dogs barking, or birds chirping. Rest on the sounds that feel good to your nervous system and soak them up.

Smell: Next, become aware of smells around you. That might be the smell of rain or cut grass. You can interact with your environment to connect with smell even more. You might pick some needles off an evergreen tree and whiff the piney scent or stop and literally smell some roses.

Taste: Notice if any tastes accompany this experience. Sometimes, you can taste fresh air in the back of your throat, or maybe you are drinking a yummy warm beverage. Notice whatever tastes are present, even if it's the turkey sandwich you just ate.

Touch: Start by noticing the temperature of your environment. You might notice the sun's warmth or the cool air. Does the air feel dry or wet? Is it hot or cold? Notice areas of your body that feel warm and others that feel cool. You might also engage with your environment through physical touch. Reach out and touch something! Hug a tree, run your hands through the grass, or pick up a rock and feel its cool and smooth texture.

As you connect to each of your five senses, slowly and deliberately, allow your autonomic nervous system to engage more deeply with the experience. Notice if you feel any shifts in your autonomic pathways as your vagus nerve responds to this practice.

Developing a Practice

We have reviewed several somatic-based strategies to stimulate and tone your vagus nerve, aiming to develop a more flexible vagal brake. The objective of these practices is to help you gain greater control over your autonomic nervous system's response to threats and stress.

These practices should not be used once, then discarded. To tone your vagus nerve effectively, it is essential to regularly engage in strategies that activate the vagal brake and enhance your neurophysiological flexibility. Although practicing these skills during moments of overwhelm can help reduce distress, the optimal approach is to incorporate them into your daily routine, even when you are not in immediate need of them. To return to our gym metaphor, visiting the gym once a month is not enough to achieve those lofty fitness goals you set on New Year's. Similarly, if you only sporadically exercise your nervous system, these skills will have minimal impact. With daily practice and intentional application, you will experience noticeable gains over time.

Highlights and Takeaways

- To gain more control and self-efficacy over your autonomic pathways, you must practice skills that tone or exercise the vagus nerve.

- A flexible vagus nerve contributes to greater emotional balance, resiliency, and stress management skills.

- Many activities and skills stimulate and tone the vagus nerve. Some covered in this chapter include yoga nidra, breathwork, mindfulness, and engaging with nature.

- Yoga nidra involves progressive body relaxation and guided imagery to experience a state of peace and calm.

- Scientific research supports breathing exercises as a way to reduce stress and overwhelm. They work the vagal brake and tone the vagus.

- Meditation can be challenging for some who are in chronic states of overwhelm. While beneficial for many, if meditation is too complicated to practice, start with mindfulness techniques.

- The autonomic nervous system also responds positively to nature. You can turn any experience with nature into a vagal exercise by focusing on your five senses.

Chapter 7

Interoception

How do you feel right now? Pause for a moment and try to answer this question.

Can you describe what you're feeling? And more than that, can you explain how you know that's what you're feeling?

For example, suppose I told you that I feel content. In that case, I can also say that I know that's how I feel because of a warm sensation in my chest, a quietness in my mind, and an overall sense of relaxation in my body. Or I can tell you that I'm feeling anxious, and I know that because my mind is scattered, my jaw is tense, and I can't sit still.

The ability to perceive and make sense of what you're feeling is called *interoception,* and it is a vital skill to develop on your journey of personal transformation and growth. Interoception is the ability to tune into the signals and sensations in your body and make sense of them. It's having an awareness of your internal landscape—the subtle fluctuations of your heartbeat, the changing rhythm of your breath, and the kaleidoscope of feelings and sensations that ebb and flow throughout the day. Interoception equips you with a whole lot of self-awareness. It also opens up a wealth of opportunities when it comes to managing stress and regulating big, messy feelings.

When we can notice feelings and bodily sensations, we are gifted with the opportunity to intervene. The more skilled we are at interoception, the more information we have available to us. And information is power when it comes to managing your nervous system. Interoception is linked to vagal functioning and an increased ability to regulate emotions, and it is a priceless skill to have on the stress management journey (Pinna et al. 2020). So, how do we develop our interoceptive powers? By learning to notice and name our internal experiences.

Let's return to my previous comment about what anxiety feels like to me. Suppose I notice those signs of anxiety creeping in because of my interoceptive abilities. In that case, I can pause and hit the brake: I can use skills to reduce the activation of my sympathetic pathway before it turns into a full-blown flurry of anxiety and panic. Interoception is the precursor to being able to cue skills to regulate. Interoception informs self-regulation. Why? Because if you're not aware of how you're feeling, how can you do anything about it?

All of the skills in this chapter focus on improving your interoceptive abilities. Like a superpower, interoception skills can help you surf the autonomic tides of your neurobiology and use techniques to calm the internal chaos. Rather than getting swept away with the current, interoceptive skills alert you that it's time to engage the vagal brake and slow autonomic reactions. The skills in this chapter will teach you how to develop your interoceptive skills and provide you with strategies to thwart autonomic defenses that needlessly spring into action.

Thoughts vs. Beliefs vs. Feelings

Did you know that thoughts and feelings are not the same thing? As a therapist, I can't tell you how many times I've asked someone what they were feeling, and they responded with a bunch of thoughts such as "I think he's a jerk!" or "I just don't know how that could have happened." While valid perspectives, these are thoughts and beliefs, not feelings.

Thoughts are processes that take place in the mind. They are the running commentary in your head. Thoughts often include opinions, reflections, analyses, and predictions. For example, the chatter running in your mind about the chore you have to do, the conversation you had the other day, and something that's going to happen tonight are all thoughts. Thoughts are like a long-winded narrative that never stops. They are the constant chatter taking place between your ears.

Beliefs are convictions we hold that shape our view and experience of the world. They tend to be all or nothing and express a truth that we hold about something or someone. For example, "I'm a loving and kind-hearted person" is a belief. "The world is out of control; that political party is bad; my mother-in-law is a pain; I have people I can trust" are all examples of beliefs. Beliefs are like mic-drop statements. They're short statements that assert a truth or a fact (whether or not they're accurate).

Feelings, on the other hand, take place in the body. While feelings are interpreted by the brain, they are separate from the mental chatter that runs 24/7 in the background of your awareness. Feelings are expressions of emotions that we experience through bodily sensations. Feelings are like a vibe or atmosphere. You know you're having a feeling because of the various bodily sensations that accompany feelings.

Learning interoception requires you to focus on your body and your feelings. While interoception might use thoughts as relevant data, interoception is founded in your bodily experience. That means it is focused mostly on physical sensations and feelings.

Let's try a little pop quiz and test your understanding of these concepts.

For each of the questions below, identify if the statement reflects a thought, belief, feeling, or body sensation. There may be more than one, so list everything that seems accurate.

1. *I'm a difficult person.*

   This is an example of a belief. It is expressed as an absolute truth.

2. *I feel fear and notice my heart is racing.*

   This is an expression of a feeling and a bodily sensation. The word fear is a feeling, and it's accompanied by a body sensation of a racing heart.

3. *I don't know what to do about this situation. Should I tell her I can make that appointment or not? I'm not sure I want to spend my time doing that, but will I upset her if I say no?*

This is an example of a thought. It's a running narrative of mental chatter.

4.   *I am excited for tonight. I deserve this.*

This is an example of a feeling mixed in with a belief! "Excited" is a feeling, and "I deserve this" is expressed as a mic-drop of truth, aka a belief.

5.   *What if I can't do it? I'm so stupid. I can't believe I did it again. I'm so embarrassed of myself and ashamed. I knew I'd mess it up. I feel like I'm going to throw up.*

This is a mixture of all of them. These words are examples of a running narrative of thoughts mixed up with beliefs ("I'm so stupid;" "I knew I'd mess it up") along with some feelings ("embarrassed;" "ashamed"). And finally, the statement "I'm going to throw up" is a body sensation.

With this awareness, try to be more reflective and self-aware of thoughts, beliefs, feelings, and body sensations. Next time you notice what you're experiencing inside, try to separate these out. When you're in a conversation with someone or watching a movie, try to parse these as people converse. This is one step to building interoceptive awareness.

The Language of Sensation

Your body has a unique language that it uses as the basis of experience and communication. It is the language of sensation. Learning to speak the language of sensation is a necessary step for growing those interoceptive superpowers.

The language of sensation does not rely upon beliefs, thoughts, or intellectual information. It is based on sensory experiences. The language of the body is founded on temperature, texture, sounds, and physical sensations. If I asked you to describe what fear feels like in your body, do you have the sensory language to do that? What about excitement, joy, love, and lust?

We only know that we have a feeling because of the sensations that make up that feeling "profile." All of your feelings have a "profile" or a set of sensations that your brain analyzes and then slaps a label on. "That is the profile of worry. I'm feeling worried." or "That is the profile of gratitude. I am feeling gratitude." What you feel in your body, where you feel it, how your body responds, the energetic description of the sensation, body temperature, heart rate, and breath patterns are all factors that collectively create a feeling profile.

Your brain interprets the sensory information it receives and then uses language and prediction to label that profile of sensations. Based on the label we place on the experience, we may have a host of associations and assumptions that come along with that profile. For example, "I'm feeling anxious, and that's a bad thing," or "I'm feeling apprehensive, and I shouldn't." While you might call a certain sensation frustration and label it a "negative emotion," your body doesn't have the same experience. To your body, frustration is just a mixture of neurobiological processes. Those processes create sensations that you label as frustration and, in return, make meaning based on your associations and lived experiences.

Growing your interoceptive skills means you have to get out of your head and into your body. That means paying attention to the sensory data points that are fueled by your autonomic pathways. Learning the language of sensation requires you to get away from thoughts that accompany a feeling profile. "Could that be the feeling of worry? Well, I really don't have anything to be worried about. It will all be okay, and I need to get over it," might be something you say to yourself, but it's probably not very helpful. We also need to get away from the beliefs we hold about our feelings. "I am a neurotic, worried person." This is not the language of sensation. This is the chatter that happens in the mind in response to feelings and sensations and blocks the pathway for personal growth.

To get out of our heads and into our bodies, we have to learn how to notice sensations and describe our internal experience. I refer to this as the skill of notice and name (Kase 2023). We have to notice the physical location of sensations in the body and be able to use language to describe or name the experience.

Learning to notice and name is a game changer when it comes to your ability to manage stress and overwhelm.

Notice and Name

In this exercise, you will learn two foundational skills of interoception: noticing the body and naming sensations. This exercise will take around twenty minutes to practice.

Settle into a quiet space free of distractions. Focus on your breath to bring your attention to your body. Take a few moments to get centered and settled.

Notice the body: The first step is learning to notice your body. Noticing your body may sound simple, but most of us forget about it throughout the day. Our fast-paced society is full of sensory stimuli that disconnect us from our bodily experience. It's all too easy to get stuck in our heads. When we live dissociated from the body, we have fewer resources to deal with stress. Learning to come home to the body and notice it is the first step of interoception.

Let's practice right now by raising awareness of the body through a progressive body scan.

There's no right or wrong way to practice this. Just notice the various spaces in your body as you read them. Try to refrain from judging your body or telling stories about your body. For example, "I hate my stomach" is not what we're going for. Instead, try to notice each bodily location and hold it in your awareness without getting sucked up into commentary.

Move through these bodily locations slowly, hovering your awareness over each for around five to ten seconds.

Read each point in the body, and try to notice just that location.

Head	Middle back
Face	Lower back
Ears	Chest
Jaw	Abdomen
Back of the neck	Pelvis
Front of the throat	Hips
Shoulders	Thighs
Arms	Shins
Hands	Calves
Upper back	Feet

Now, observe your entire body.

Breathe for a few minutes as you hold awareness of your entire body.

Name your sensations: *The next step is to develop body-based language. Body-based language is based on sensory language rather than thoughts and feelings. Sensory language includes words such as hot, cold, light, heavy, sharp, dull, smooth, flat, loud, and quiet, to name a few. It is based on sensation and, therefore, focuses on qualities of temperature, energy, sound, smell, texture, and so forth.*

Name one feeling that you are aware of at this moment. Remember, feelings and thoughts are not the same. "I don't know if I'm doing this exercise right" is a thought, whereas "confused" is a feeling. You might be in more than one feeling right now, which is the case for most of us most of the time. But pick just one feeling to focus on.

Next, answer the following questions for the feeling you identified, moving through one at a time.

Where do I feel this in my body?

What color is this sensation?

What temperature is this sensation?

What kind of energy does this sensation have?

How much weight does this sensation have?

Is there a sound that goes along with this sensation?

What other words describe this sensation?

Now, reorient to your environment and transition away from this work. Write down any final reflections that stand out to you here.

This exercise helps you get in tune with the feelings and sensations that are constantly taking place inside your body. This is a useful skill to practice throughout the day, as doing so will help make interoception second nature for you. The more attuned you become to the sensations that are taking place in your body, the more attuned you can be to your nervous system's needs.

Automatic Narratives

Did you know that your thoughts change depending on which pathway is most activated? That's right! Your thoughts and thinking are very much influenced by the state of your autonomic nervous system (Dana 2021).

Call to mind the qualities of your sympathetic pathway. Think about all of the feelings and body sensations that go along with this pathway in times of stress and overwhelm. When you're feeling all of that mobilizing energy, what tends to happen with your thoughts? Are they calm and cool? Or do they tend to shift to being more anxious, obsessive, or even catastrophic?

Now, consider what happens to your thoughts when your dorsal pathway is activated. When you feel shut down, collapsed, and depressed, what is the quality of your thoughts there? Are they happy and full of sunshine? Probably not.

Last but not least, consider your thought patterns when you're rooted in ventral. When you feel grounded, at ease, and peaceful, what are your thoughts like?

I imagine you noticed a significant difference between each pathway. That's because our autonomic state informs our *automatic narratives*. Your automatic narratives can be considered the quality of thinking that automatically takes over based on your autonomic state.

If you can become aware of your automatic narratives, you have an opportunity to notice, name your state, and intervene. For example, when I notice my thoughts are slow, heavy, and sad, I know that my body is in a state of dorsal shutdown. When I notice this, I can cue a skill to manage my overwhelm and increase my connection to the ventral pathway. This can help regulate my autonomic state and bring me back to a more balanced and calm state.

On the other hand, when I notice my thoughts are focused on productivity, achievement, and success, I know that my body is in a state of sympathetic arousal. In this case, I may need to take a break, engage in some self-care activities, or practice mindfulness to bring myself back into a more relaxed state.

Being aware of our thought patterns and how they relate to our underlying autonomic state can be incredibly powerful. It allows us to have agency over our reactions and responses rather than being controlled by them. By understanding the connection between our thoughts and our autonomic state, we can learn to regulate our nervous system and create a more balanced and harmonious internal state.

My Automatic Narratives

Let's take some time to learn your automatic narratives so you can use that awareness for good. This exercise may take you fifteen to twenty minutes.

Find a place to sit quietly with something to write with.

Take a few intentional breaths to get centered. Set an intention to be curious and learn.

We'll explore each of your autonomic pathways and the narratives that they automatically activate for you. Move through each of the pathways outlined below, one at a time.

Sympathetic Narratives

Call to mind all of the qualities that accompany your sympathetic pathway when it's cued in response to danger and stress. As you hold that awareness, complete the following prompts:

> *What do I think about myself in this pathway?*
>
> *What do I think about other people in this pathway?*
>
> *What do I think about the state of the world in this pathway?*

Dorsal Narratives

Now, bring to mind all of the qualities associated with dorsal shutdown. When dorsal's immobilizing qualities are activated in response to danger or stress, what happens to your automatic narratives?

> *What do I think about myself in this pathway?*
>
> *What do I think about other people in this pathway?*
>
> *What do I think about the state of the world in this pathway?*

Ventral Narratives

Finally, consider the quality of your thoughts when you are grounded in the safety of ventral. What are your automatic thoughts like in this pathway?

> *What do I think about myself in this pathway?*
>
> *What do I think about other people in this pathway?*
>
> *What do I think about the state of the world in this pathway?*

Reflect on the narratives you have uncovered with the following questions:

> *Which automatic narratives influence me the most?*

How do these narratives impact me, my loved ones, and the way I perceive the world?

Which narratives are helpful? Are there any that are harmful?

Based on this exercise, what insights can I take away about my automatic narratives?

To continue this work, set an intention to be more aware of your narratives throughout the day. You can set a reminder to check in with these narratives throughout the day.

Learning to identify and spot your automatic narratives can be another method for tracking your autonomic blueprint. Your automatic narratives hold information and data and can be used in a number of ways if you learn to tune into them. For example, suppose I notice my sympathetic narrative as part of my experience. In that case, I can use the scanning interoception exercise or RESET technique in chapter 4 to assess the validity of the narrative and find some emotional balance. The narrative can be an indicator it's time to hit the brakes.

Recognize that if thoughts change in relationship to your autonomic pathways, that means that those dorsal and sympathetic charged narratives likely aren't true. Rather, your thinking is colored by the state of your nervous system. If the thoughts you held in those stress responses were actually true, they wouldn't change depending on how you feel in the moment. Truth is truth and doesn't change depending on the state of your neurobiology. Therefore, recognizing that your thinking patterns tend to shift alongside your autonomic pathways can offer you a dose of reality when you need it.

Challenging Assumptions

The narratives that our autonomic pathways can activate have the potential to cause a lot of suffering. When stress responses take over, our minds can run away with us. We all suffer from a chatterbox of a mind that constantly runs commentary, feeds us narratives, daydreams, has random thoughts, and forms opinions. That's what your mind is supposed to do.

Our mind and body maintain a constant feedback loop. Our autonomic nervous system may react to a cue of danger and move us into a protective pathway. That pathway then feeds the automatic narrative. As we sit there thinking about how unlikeable we think we are and how terrible the world is, those thoughts feed back into our autonomic pathway. They become fuel for the fire. The autonomic nervous system responds, the mind responds, and around and around we go.

There are many points of intervention in this feedback loop. Techniques we discussed in chapter 6 mostly focus on the body. However, we can also use cognitive strategies to calm the reaction in the mind. One way to do this is to challenge our assumptions.

We can regain control over autonomic responses and engage the vagal brake by double-checking our thoughts and beliefs about a situation (Denson et al. 2011). A way to say, "Hold up. Am I thinking right? Could there be other explanations? Where are the facts?" *Challenging assumptions* does exactly this, as it challenges your perspective or thinking by seeking out alternative explanations. For example, when someone cuts in front of you in line, an emotionally driven response would be to assume that they did that because they are a rude and terrible person. If this is your snap judgment, that belief has the potential to charge up an automatic reaction. You may experience a flood of anger, get confrontational, or sit there quietly stewing with smoke coming out your ears. Your autonomic nervous system is behaving automatically, and it's causing your mind to believe some things that aren't true. Sometimes, you literally need to check your nervous system.

To challenge this situation requires you to hit your vagal brake, slow down the emotional rollercoaster, and consider alternative explanations. Learning to slow your response requires you to put some restraint on the autonomic pathways charging up, giving your brain time to reassess the situation. You might notice that the person who cut in front of you is seeing impaired, so they literally couldn't see you! Or perhaps you observe that they have a screaming child on their hip and are understandably a bit checked out from their surroundings. You gently inform them, "Hello, the line actually starts back here." Embarrassed, they apologize and quickly move to the back of the line. Turns out they weren't intentionally trying to snub you, defy societal line-forming norms, or be rude to anyone.

Our nervous system is designed to protect us, and because of this, we have something called a *negativity bias*. The negativity bias is the tendency for "adults to display a negativity bias, or the propensity to attend to, learn from, and use negative information far more than positive information" (Vaish et al. 2008). The negativity bias is why we're so quick to focus on the negative, disregard the positive, and jump to conclusions. As neuroception is always scanning for cues to predict and protect you from danger, it makes sense that your nervous system would be biased to look for threats. However, our autonomic nervous system can take it too far and keep us from seeing the nonthreatening alternatives, or reality for that matter.

Here are a few other common scenarios in which challenging assumptions could be beneficial:

- Your boss shares some critical feedback on a performance review. You personalize the feedback and take it to mean you're a terrible, horrible person and shut down for the rest of the week. The truth of the matter may be that you need to be held accountable for missing a deadline, and this feedback is an opportunity to improve.

- Your mother-in-law gives you a strange look at the dinner table. You interpret it to mean that she thinks poorly of you and your cooking, and you angrily stew for the rest of the meal. The truth may actually be that she has indigestion, and that look was the look of gas.

- You are staying at a hotel. You feel a little anxious, given it's a new place and you're by yourself. You hear some loud voices in the hall, and your brain starts playing out scenarios in which you are abducted and held for ransom. You end up getting four hours of sleep and feeling terrible the next day. The fact is, the loud noises were just kids playing tag in the hall.

Challenging assumptions is not a means to bypass danger cues that should be taken seriously. Yes, sometimes the loud noise is something to be concerned about, and the strange look is a sign that someone is about to cause you bodily harm. However, given that our brain tends to err on the side of danger, checking your automatic reaction for accuracy can be helpful in a lot of situations. Autonomic defenses represent complex neurobiological processes that can be hard to check for accuracy sometimes. They are your survival instincts, so of course, it's hard to override them. However, learning to challenge your assumptions is a means of responding rather than reacting to a situation.

Identify Alternatives

Next time you notice a rise in unpleasant sensations and activation of autonomic defenses, try to pause and ask yourself the following questions:

- What is the assumption or prediction my brain is making? (e.g., I'm in danger; I'm a terrible person; They don't like me; They are a horrible human being.)

- Could I be wrong?

- Are there alternative explanations?

- What is my evidence for this assumption or prediction?

Maybe

I have studied Buddhism and yoga philosophy for several decades now. I have found a wealth of useful strategies for not only regulating my neurobiology but also making sense of the complexities of life. There is a specific story I learned some time ago that has profoundly influenced my way of thinking, which in turn has supported my emotional regulation skills. This story highlights the importance of refraining from quick assumptions and conclusions. Because our autonomic pathways and automatic narratives can so strongly influence our perception, this story is a good reminder to slow down and check yourself.

Once upon a time, there was a farmer whose horse ran away. His neighbors came by and expressed their sadness for his situation. "We're so sorry your horse ran away! This is terrible!" The farmer simply replied, "Maybe."

The next day, the horse returned. But it wasn't alone! It showed up with several other horses by its side. His neighbors came right back over and, with joy, said, "How fortunate and wonderful! You have more horses than you did before!" The farmer replied, "Maybe."

The next morning, the farmer's son tried to ride one of the new horses. The horse bucked him off, and he broke his leg. The neighbors again expressed their condolences. "What a tragedy!" And again, the farmer replied, "Maybe."

The next day, a group of soldiers came through town, recruiting young men for the military. Seeing the boy's broken leg, they passed him by. "You are SO lucky!" the farmer's neighbors exclaimed when they heard the news. "Maybe," said the farmer.

The wisdom of this story is that it highlights that we never truly know how something will pan out, yet we are often quick to judge things as good or bad, lucky or unlucky. We can thank neuroception and our natural biases for this. After all, that's just your internal surveillance system making quick calls based on the information available to it. However, as we can learn from this story, there are many times when those quick appraisals aren't accurate.

Next time you notice yourself making assumptions about whether or not something is good or bad, remember this story and simply whisper to yourself, "Maybe." When we remind ourselves that the future has yet to unfold and that everything is susceptible to change, we can regain some control over automatic reactions to events and circumstances that we quickly judge to be dangerous, unfortunate, or disastrous. Reminding yourself "maybe" is a way to get back to reality and calm the internal freak out with a dose of ventral.

Change the Volume

Once you learn to identify your autonomic responses, feelings, and body sensations, you have a greater opportunity to use skills to flexibly maneuver between autonomic pathways. This means you get better at using emotion regulation skills to reduce stress and overwhelm. While our autonomic pathways may quickly react and we have limited ability to control them, we have considerable ability to respond to our reactions. Consciously using skills and techniques to work with your vagus nerve and autonomic blueprint is what emotion regulation is all about!

I sometimes think of my autonomic nervous system like a volume dial on a stereo. And I have the power to change the volume. When the volume is turned up too "high," I associate this with my sympathetic pathway being revved up and on full alert. I might be experiencing the qualities of anxiety and restlessness, have a racing heart, and feel incredibly mobilized. All of that mobilizing energy is "loud," and my goal is to use skills to reduce the volume to a tolerable level.

Similarly, when the volume is too "low," I experience the immobilizing and flattening experience of dorsal shutdown. I might be completely void of energy, flat and down in the dumps. In these situations, I need to turn up the volume so I can get back to life and feel good.

You too can use skills to engage your vagus nerve and change the volume of your autonomic pathways. But to do so, you have to know which skills help you change the volume.

Turn Down the Volume

When you notice you're feeling the pressure and noise of sympathetic overwhelm, it's time to turn down the volume. You can do this by calling on skills that "turn down the volume" inside. When the volume's too loud, turn to skills and activities that calm or dissipate the intensity of that mobilized sympathetic pathway.

There is no finite set of skills nor any right or wrong techniques when it comes to turning down the volume. Each of us is unique, and therefore, you will have an individualized array of noise-reducing techniques that will likely change over time. Sometimes, we need movement and energy to dissipate sympathetic mobilization, while other times, we might need stillness. Focus on techniques that engage your vagal brake and, in doing so, increase your connection to your ventral pathway.

Some of my techniques to turn down the volume involve quiet walks in nature, yoga, getting a massage, taking a bath, or the physiological sigh described in chapter 6. But sometimes what my nervous system is asking me for is a way to discharge all of that loud energy. In those times, I may go to the gym and do a hard workout. I might dance, yell in the privacy of my car, or turn on some music that matches my mood. Rather than focusing on a set of specific skills, focus on the feelings and sensations in your body and what they may intuitively need.

Take some time to create a list of strategies to turn down the volume. Keep adding to the list as you find new things that work. It's useful to write these down now so that when you're at a breaking point or overwhelmed, you have a list to turn to. That sympathetic overwhelm can prevent your brain from remembering these strategies. Write these down and keep them somewhere handy so that next time you need to turn down the volume, you have a menu of techniques to choose from.

Turn Up the Volume

While turning down the volume will help you move out of sympathetic fight-or-flight states, learning to turn up the volume can help you move out of dorsal shutdown states.

When our dorsal pathway gets activated due to fear and danger, it can leave us feeling like the volume is turned down way too low. We might experience pain, hollowness, and loneliness as we collapse within and check out from feeling our bodies.

When you're in this state, the way to turn up the volume is typically found in movement and connection. I get it. Movement is sometimes the last thing you want to do when you're in dorsal shutdown, but it is a sure way to turn that volume up. Make yourself move, even if you don't want to. Turn on some music, dance around, and sing. Do twenty jumping jacks. Go for a brisk walk. Play with your dog. All of these activities increase your heart rate as they engage with your vagus nerve, which moves you out of dorsal shutdown.

Connection with safe and compassionate people or with sweet and cuddly fur babies is also a great way to crank up the volume. While dorsal states may make us feel like we want nothing to do with anyone else, make yourself reach out and connect to someone. Phone a friend, go out in public and intentionally make eye contact and smile at people, or make a play date at the dog park. Connection can be magical and is a powerful strategy for turning up the volume when you're stuck in dorsal shutdown.

Take some time to create a list of strategies to turn up the volume. These strategies include mindfulness, meditation, movement, connection, or anything at all that has or could work for you. Remember to experiment and add to the list as you navigate the volume changes of life. Keeping this list somewhere you can easily access can help you navigate those heavy times with more ease.

Highlights and Takeaways

- This chapter focused on techniques to hit the vagal brake in moments of emotional overwhelm.

- Mind-body techniques are incredibly helpful skills for this purpose!

- Interoception is the ability to tune into bodily signals and sensations and is linked to vagal functioning and emotion regulation. Interoception is the ability to notice and name what you feel and sense in your body.

- Thoughts, beliefs, and feelings are all different but related. Learning to decipher the difference is an important starting point for learning interoception.

- We reviewed the language of the body and honed your interoceptive skills by learning to describe bodily sensations.

- Learning to challenge assumptions, reappraise situations, and
  seek alternative explanations is a means to engage the vagal
  brake and calm an overwhelmed nervous system.

- Learning to observe and challenge your automatic narratives is
  a great regulation strategy. Noticing your automatic narratives
  is also a great strategy for influencing your emotional state.

- Learning to "change the volume" is a metaphor I use to work
  with autonomic pathways. Creating a list of strategies to change
  the volume in your nervous system is a skillful way to do this.

- You can "change the volume" of your nervous system with
  awareness and skillful application of strategies to regulate autonomic pathways.

Chapter 8

Your Social Engagement System

Polyvagal theory offers a wealth of insight into how our nervous system functions and responds to danger and safety as well as what it needs to function optimally. But this book would be incomplete if we didn't discuss an additional important insight that the theory teaches us: the power of connection.

"To connect and coregulate with others is our biological imperative" (Porges 2017). This quote from Stephen Porges is a great segue into something called the *social engagement system*. The social engagement system is what allows us to form relationships and connections. It is, in part, made possible by the vagus nerve, and it's a super important concept when it comes to using the wisdom of polyvagal to better your life.

You, dear human, are wired for connection. Your nervous system is designed to be social, make friends, fall in love, and crave connection. No matter how introverted you might be, no one does well living in isolation. Humans are social creatures, and this helps us get through life. Social bonds allow us to find safety in numbers, form societies, learn, and grow. Unlike animals like sea turtles who never meet their mother, humans require connection to not only survive but thrive. And we can partially thank the vagus nerve for helping us form and benefit from relationships.

Remember the first time you got your heart karate-kicked by love? It sucked, didn't it? I remember the first boyfriend who broke my heart. I was sixteen years old, and I thought Craig was the love of my life.

Those young days of adolescent hormones and the intoxication of lust made me think that he was the real deal. But after a whole four months of dating (I know, such a long stint we had), Craig pulled a vanishing act. Yup. He made like a ghost and stopped talking to me. I remember the angst I felt as I sat alone in my bedroom, writing his name over and over in my diary with hearts and arrows, spilling tears onto the college-ruled pages. The pain I felt when he passed by me in the school hallways without acknowledging my existence was a visceral experience. Craig was done with me, and my nervous system felt confused and abandoned by a boy for the first time in my life. It was gut wrenching.

If it weren't for the fact that I'm a human with a nervous system wired to connect, I might have called it quits after Craig. I might have said, "You know what, this is too painful. Screw dating." But because my nervous system is designed to form social bonds, I decided to get back into the dating game. I got my heart broken again and again and again and again until my early 30s. I'm now married to an amazing man who would never ghost me but still might break my heart one day. People change, divorce happens, and we all eventually die. So, at some point, one of us in this marriage will likely break the other person's heart. And even though there's all that risk, and the risk of that heart-break only grows the more attached and connected we become, the power of love overrides the risk. That's the power of the social engagement system.

The social engagement system isn't solely about falling in love. It plays a role in every single relationship you have, be it with partners, family members, pets, or colleagues. Every time you come into contact with a mammal, the social engagement system plays a role in how connected you are with that creature and how you feel about that creature. Consider how anxiety-producing a toxic boss can be. Or how warm you feel inside when you feel validated by a friend. Or the happiness that floods you when you come home to an ecstatic dog about to wiggle its butt off with joy. All of that is made possible by your neurobiology and vagus nerve.

Relationships are like water for us. You simply can't go without them if you want to thrive. When we feel safe with someone, we are capable of amazing things. Likewise, when someone feels safe with us, we offer them an invaluable resource. On the flip side, when we feel unsafe with someone or someone feels unsafe with us, things get really complicated, messy, conflictual, and even dangerous. Our ability to form safe relationships is, in part, made possible by the vagus nerve. So, let's dive into the power of our social engagement system and explore its relationship to emotional wellness.

Safety First

All healthy relationships are based on one key ingredient. Safety.

Consider all that you have learned about the role safety plays when it comes to your autonomic pathways. When you feel safe, you can thrive. Safety allows you to anchor in your ventral pathway, which is where you can be your best self. When we feel safe with another person, we can do several important things.

First, when we have enough safety with someone, we can be a good friend, partner, and human. When we feel safe, we can laugh, play, make jokes, be good listeners, and share vulnerable stories. We can be creative, collaborate, and problem solve. All of that is possible with safety. Safety makes for very productive and resourceful relationships, family units, teams, and societies.

Safety also gives us more resources for protection. Have you ever heard the saying "safety in numbers"? Having a pack or team or even just one other person around you that you feel safe with ups your chances of survival. When we humans were living in caves, safety with others might mean you could rest, trusting that one of your sisters or brothers was watching the cave entrance and tending to the fire. When SWAT teams enter buildings, they enter together, watching each other's backs. And when you're sick and can't get to the store for medicine, safety is having someone to call on to help you get through a rough patch.

Safety also allows us to be vulnerable. Consider how much safety you need with someone to share some of your darkest, most painful, and most uncomfortable thoughts and stories. Most of us find it hard to be vulnerable because vulnerability in and of itself doesn't feel very safe. But when someone meets our vulnerability with compassion, kindness, and care, we can share our story and reduce the loneliness we're feeling. This is not to say that we can't form bonds and relationships with people who aren't safe. Domestic violence, codependency, trauma bonds, and showing allegiance to your perpetrator are all examples of how confused our social engagement system can get. And while you can certainly form relationships with those you don't feel safe with, those relationships probably don't contribute to your health and wellness. They are rather a likely threat to your physical and psychological health due to the constant stress, worry, fear, and danger they present with. However, we get stuck in those unhealthy dynamics because the need for connection overrides the danger of staying. We are wired to connect, and therefore, sometimes, our drive to connect drives us into relationships that aren't ideal for us. So, while we might find ourselves connected to someone who isn't good for us, for a relationship to contribute to our resiliency, true and consistent safety must be present. Without safety, that unsafe relationship will cause you a host of physical and psychological forms of suffering because your autonomic pathways of defense are constantly activated.

The Power of Safety

Let's rev up some introspection time and examine just how important safety is in your relationships. In this exercise, we will explore how safe and unsafe relationships affect you and your nervous system. This will take around fifteen minutes. I recommend you pull up your autonomic blueprint, which you reviewed in chapter 3, for easy reference.

Find a quiet and comfortable space where you can reflect without interruption. Have a notebook or journal ready for this practice.

Take a few breaths and center yourself. You might close your eyes and focus on your body for a minute or so and allow yourself to settle.

Now let's explore people who activate your autonomic pathways:

Call to mind someone who activates your dorsal pathway. This might be someone from the past or someone in your present life who you feel shut down and withdrawn around. Someone who you feel small, timid, or insecure around. Reflect on who that person is and what factors cue your system into dorsal as best as you can identify. How does this or has this person influenced your life? How do you feel about this person?

Now, call into mind someone who activates your sympathetic pathway. Someone who causes your nervous system to feel mobilized, anxious, and worked up. Reflect on who that person is and what factors cue your system into sympathetic, as best as you can identify. How does this or has this person influenced your life? How do you feel about this person?

Last, reflect on someone with whom you feel safe and connected. This is someone with whom you can be vulnerable, laugh and play, and bring joy and peace into your life. This person brings your ventral pathway to life. Reflect on who that person is and what factors cue your system into ventral as best as you can identify. How does this person influence your life?

Based on your reflections, answer the following questions:

How do these relationships contribute to or hinder my emotional and physical health?

What is the cost of relationships that chronically activate my dorsal and sympathetic pathways?

What are the benefits of relationships that support my connection to ventral?

Before you wrap up this exercise, promise yourself to stay curious and reflect on the quality of your relationships and how they influence your vagus nerve.

The Superpower of Coregulation

Did you know that you have a superpower? It's called *coregulation*. Coregulation is the ability to regulate someone else. Yup! Your nervous system can rub off on someone else's.

When you place a hand on a crying friend's shoulder or rock an infant to sleep, you are providing coregulation. When your colleague brings you some chocolate and says, "Looks like you could use a pick-me-up," they're offering you coregulation. And when your dog puts their head in your lap when you're crying, they're trying to coregulate you. Coregulation is a truly powerful and fascinating thing that we social creatures, especially humans and canines, offer each other. And when you learn to use it with intentionality, you harness this super-power and make the world a safer place.

Coregulation also helps us to produce oxytocin, which is sometimes referred to as our "cuddle chemical." It's a feel-good hormone you might get a dump of after orgasm, a big belly laugh, or snuggling closely with a loved one. Oxytocin plays an important role in shaping early neural circuits, forming the infant-mother bond, and influencing our ability to form healthy social relationships (Muscatelli et al. 2022). Your body was literally designed to benefit from relationships, as evidenced by this natural, feel-good drug you make in response to a safe connection.

Coregulation paves the way to self-regulation. Depending on how much or how little regulation you had as a child has an effect on how much capacity you have to regulate yourself as an adult. If you had a lot of coregulation in childhood, you likely learned skills and behaviors that helped you regulate your autonomic pathways and build vagal tone. While many other factors can influence your development, coregulation is one of the most important. While your mother probably didn't think, "I'm rocking my child, and in doing so, I am helping them build vagal tone and autonomic resiliency," on a neurobiological level, that's what she was doing.

Do not take this as a doomsday message. Many people reading this had less-than-ideal parents and caregivers. That's probably part of the reason you feel like you need the information in this book! I promise you're not sentenced to a life void of vagal flexibility and resiliency.

Luckily, the nervous system has something called *neuroplasticity*. Neuroplasticity is simply your nervous system's ability to remodel itself. Pretty cool, huh? As we learn new things, our nervous system is "modified by the environmental input" (Innocenti 2022). Our brains and nervous systems are constantly changing and reshaping themselves. You certainly don't have the same brain as an adult as you did as an infant. And you develop new neural networks as you learn new skills and behaviors. The ability of your nervous system to change and adapt means that even if your childhood was sucky, you can still learn skills as an adult to manage your autonomic pathways better. Using the power of coregulation for good is one way you can do that.

Coregulation takes place through the many ways that we express safety, care, and comfort to each other. We can offer coregulation with the words we use, the tone of our voice, gestures, facial expressions, and body language. It might be a timely sigh and soft eyes that communicate care and compassion. Or maybe it's a warm hug that reminds you you're not alone. Or perhaps it's the shoulder to cry on, the words "I'm so sorry you're going through this," that communicate empathy and care for someone else.

You might consider coregulation to be like throwing someone a lifeline when they're flooded with sympathetic overwhelm or tanking in dorsal shutdown. It's a way for us to support each other by sharing our neurobiological resources. Coregulation often doesn't take much—a little can go a long way. With the knowledge of coregulation, you can use this skill with those you love and seek it out when you need some regulation yourself.

Let's examine some examples of coregulation so you can get a better picture of all the small and big ways we can coregulate each other.

- Smiling at someone and expressing genuine care with your tone of voice and words.

- Offering your partner a hug when they're feeling down.

- Comforting your pet or child when they're scared.

- Calling a friend when you need a pick-me-up.

- Speaking to someone in a calm and soothing voice when they're angry and worked up.

- Leaning in when a friend is crying or sharing a vulnerable story.

- Saying, "You're okay," with a warm tone of voice as your child gets a shot at the doctor.

By simply observing interactions, you can develop a keen awareness of the many ways that we coregulate each other, in big and small ways. Watch for the ways that you spontaneously offer coregulation to others and vice versa. With more awareness of the power of correlation, you will start to see it everywhere. And you can start to use it intentionally.

Your Nervous System Is Contagious

To feel safe and create safety with others, you need your vagus nerve to join the party. Without that vagal brake working its magic, you might fly off the handle when you feel frustrated with your teenager. Or you might faint and pass out when you experience conflict with your boss. You might be unable to squash that urge to give someone the finger and yell a few expletives when they snag your parking spot. Without your vagus nerve allowing you access to your ventral pathway, you might send some scary signals to coworkers, your family, and a stranger at the grocery store.

My ability to be a good friend, partner, and dog mom tanks when I'm outside of my ventral pathway. When my sympathetic pathway is revved up full throttle, I have a hard time listening, focusing, and managing my anxiety. On the other end of the spectrum, when I'm in dorsal shutdown, the last thing I want to do is hang out with people. I'm more likely to cancel dinner plans or not respond to a call or text. I'm sure you can relate to this on some level. This change in behavior isn't because I'm a bad person, I'm a jerk, or I don't care. It's because of my neurobiology. The hard truth is that your autonomic pathways change your mood and your capacity for connection. You just aren't the best version of yourself when you're outside of your ventral pathway.

As we consider how impactful autonomic pathways are on our relationships, we cannot dismiss the implications for societies, communities, and humankind as a whole. Consider how a world leader's lack of autonomic regulation impacts the decisions they make about policy and how they handle conflict. Consider how a police officer who is chronically stuck in sympathetic overwhelm is more likely to perceive people as hostile and react rather than respond. Consider how a parent with years of unresolved trauma and a lack of coregulation in their childhood can perpetuate that with their child.

Relationships can be the best or the worst thing for us depending on how safe and regulated we are with each other. Because we can so easily influence each other's nervous systems, we will forever and always be interconnected as a species. No matter where you were born, what color your skin is, who you love, how much money you make, who you voted for, or what your religious beliefs are—you are part of the fabric of humankind. Polyvagal theory and the social engagement system make this glaringly obvious. As creatures designed to form social bonds, we have the power to use those social bonds for good. But, if we show up to our relationships with our autonomic pathways out of whack, our dysregulation can send ripples to everyone around us. The state of your neurobiology is contagious. So, be mindful of what you're spreading.

Autonomic Pathways and My Social System

Consider how good a friend, partner, parent, and colleague you can be when you're activated in sympathetic mobilization or dorsal shutdown due to stress, fear, or danger. Because these pathways influence so many bodily systems, it's normal and natural to recognize that you're not your best self when your defensive pathways take over. Autonomic pathways influence our capacity to listen, show interest, convey empathy, remember important events like someone's birthday, soothe someone else when they're dysregulated, and send cues of safety. Use this exercise to self-reflect and get a better understanding of how people might experience you when you're stressed out or shut down.

Find a quiet space to sit and focus for ten to twenty minutes. Grab a journal and a pen.

First, get centered. Take a few cleansing breaths and bring your awareness to your body.

Give yourself permission to be curious and honest with yourself. This exercise isn't about beating yourself up for being a bad friend or parent when you're emotionally dysregulated. Everyone is a less-than-ideal version of themselves when outside of their ventral pathway! With awareness comes the opportunity to change and use skills to hit the brakes.

Move through each of the three pathways, starting with dorsal, then sympathetic, and finally ventral. Answer the following questions for each pathway.

Start with the dorsal pathway and answer all of the questions below. Then, answer all of the questions for the sympathetic pathway, followed by ventral.

Call the pathway you're focused on to mind. You might refer to your autonomic blueprint from chapter 3. Connect with the qualities of that pathway, and explore the following questions:

What kind of a listener am I when this pathway is activated?

What happens to my ability to feel and convey empathy and compassion when this pathway is activated?

Are there common descriptions people use to describe their experience of me when this pathway is activated? For example, "you're so defensive," or "you're self-absorbed," or "I don't think you are listening."

How kind am I to the people I care about when this pathway is activated?

How interested am I in relationships when this pathway is activated?

Suppose I experienced myself like someone else did when this pathway was activated. What words might I use to describe how social and personable I was?

Anything else that stands out to you?

Repeat these questions for each of the three pathways.

Once you've explored all three pathways, ask yourself, "What kind of friend, partner, and colleague do I want to be?" Write down a few sentences or words describing how you'd like others to experience you.

Which pathway makes it possible to be that person?

Wrap up with any final reflections or intentions you'd like to set following this exercise. Use this knowledge with intentionality and increase your level of self-awareness as you relate and connect with those around you.

Mapping Your Support System

Building a strong support system is essential for emotional well-being and navigating the ups and downs of life. This self-help exercise is designed to help you identify and reflect on your safe and supportive relationships. By mapping out your support system, you can gain insights into the people who contribute positively to your life and support your growth and wellness. Note this exercise is not limited to people. Be sure to consider your supportive furry friends in this, too! Animals and pets are incredibly therapeutic for us and can sometimes be the most supportive creatures in our lives (Ortmeyer and Katzel 2020).

This exercise requires a piece of paper, a pen, and about twenty minutes.

1. On a piece of paper, draw three concentric circles similar to the image below. You'll be writing things inside the circles, so make them as large as you can.

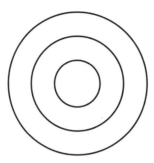

2. Write your name in the center circle.

3. The second circle represents your primary support circle. This is your closest group of individuals who provide you with love, guidance, and encouragement. They may include family members, friends, significant others, or pets.

4. In the third circle, write down the names of those who have a positive impact on your life but may not be as close to you as those in your primary support circle. These could be mentors, teachers, colleagues, friends, neighbors, or extended family.

5. Now, on a separate sheet of paper, write down all of the names that you listed in your primary support circle. Reflect on the following questions for each person you listed in your primary circle:

    a. What words do I use to describe this person/animal?

    b. Why did I place them in my primary support circle?

    c. How do they contribute to my life?

6. Do the same for your outer circle of support. List the names of everyone you placed in your outer circle and answer the following:

   a. How does this individual contribute to my well-being?

   b. Why did I add them to my outer circle?

   c. How do they contribute to my life?

7. Now, consider the following question for each individual on your map: How does this individual influence my autonomic pathways?

Take a moment to check in with your emotions as you reflect on each relationship. What do you feel as you observe your support system? Do you feel a sense of gratitude or appreciation? Or is something missing? Do you need to grow your support system to feel safe and more fulfilled?

It's also normal to notice gaps in your support map. If you're feeling like your support map could use a little TLC, that's not a bad thing! Making new friends is 100 percent possible. With technology at your disposal, you have an entire world to search for friends. Volunteer, find a group on Meetup.com, reach out to someone you haven't connected with in a long time, or find an online group. If you are craving more connection, you have to make it happen. Unfortunately, no group of people is going to show up at your door and say, "We heard you needed friends. So here we are."

Sometimes, this exercise can bring up a sense of loss if we're grieving someone. Or we may feel a lack of support in our system, and we're reminded of how lonely we are. It's okay to feel those feelings. That's your autonomic blueprint responding to the work you just did. But what your support system looks like today is not a prediction of what it will look like in a year. You are capable of forming new relationships because you're human and you have a social engagement system. And guess what? Every other human has a social engagement system, too. So, making friends is something you and everyone else are wired for. Try not to get hung up on loss or absence, and use this exercise to help inspire growth and change in your life.

This exercise is a tool for self-discovery and can serve as a visual representation of the current state of your support system. Regularly revisit and update your support map as your relationships evolve. By intentionally nurturing safe and supportive connections, you can build a robust support system that contributes to your well-being.

Cultivating Compassion: Metta Meditation

In chapter 6, you learned the heart-focused practice inspired by the Buddhist practice of metta meditation. Metta comes from the Buddhist tradition and means "loving-kindness" or "benevolence." Metta meditations focus on growing compassion for yourself, others, and even people you don't like. It is a wonderful way to stimulate your vagus nerve and connect with your social engagement system. You can access the audio recording of this practice in the link shared in chapter 2.

This exercise takes about ten to fifteen minutes depending on your speed. I recommend you find a comfortable seat in a space free from distractions.

Sit in a comfortable posture, with your hands resting on your knees or in your lap. You can also practice this lying down.

Begin by taking a few mindful breaths to center yourself. Breathe in through your nose and exhale through your mouth, releasing tension.

Begin this practice by focusing on yourself. As you visualize and connect with yourself, silently repeat the following phrases:

"May I be happy."

"May I be healthy."

"May I be safe."

"May I have peace."

Repeat this three times.

Next, extend your attention to your loved ones, family, or friends. Think of those you identified on your map of support, the exercise just before this one. Allow these individuals to float through your awareness as you repeat the following:

"May you be happy."

"May you be healthy."

"May you be safe."

"May you have peace."

Repeat this three times.

Now, call in someone who challenges you. Someone you're frustrated with or don't like. Think of that individual and say the following words:

"May you be happy."

"May you be healthy."

"May you be safe."

"May you have peace."

Repeat this three times.

Finally, expand your awareness to all beings on this planet. Envision all of the creatures on this Earth, big and small, and say the following:

"May you be happy."

"May you be healthy."

"May you be safe."

"May you have peace."

Repeat this three times.

Allow the words to float away, and return your awareness to your breath and body. Take a moment to notice anything that has changed, and slowly come back to your present environment.

A Social Pick-Me-Up

By recognizing the innate capacity of your nervous system to be social and form bonds, you can use your social engagement system as a lifeline when you're in a funk. Your social engagement system not only sends information to those around you but also receives information. And the information your system receives influences your pathways.

Consider how being around someone who's always doom and gloom or who is constantly gossiping about others can be a real buzzkill. But on the flip side, consider how someone's good mood can also influence your own mood.

You can use your social engagement system for a quick pick-me-up next time you're feeling the pangs of sympathetic overdrive or dorsal collapse. Here are some strategies to get a dose of ventral and find some regulation in times that you need it.

- Smile: Sometimes all you need to do is flash your pearly whites to get a spark of goodness. Make eye contact with a stranger and send them a big smile. Watch what happens when they return the smile and gesture.

- Give a compliment: For most of us, getting an unexpected compliment can feel like a nice surprise. Compliment someone and see what happens inside your system. It can be a big or small compliment, but make it genuine. You might compliment the grocery clerk's sneakers, tell your colleague how much you appreciate their constant supply of chocolate, or tell your child how incredibly proud you are of them for cleaning their room. The goal here isn't to go fishing and seek out a compliment for yourself. The simple act of selflessly giving someone a genuine compliment is a great way to activate your social engagement system and get a boost of good vibes.

- Give thanks: Take time to share your gratitude and thanks for someone. This is like giving a compliment but to the nth degree. Be honest and genuine and give a truly heartfelt thanks to someone who could use some recognition. You might send a text to your sister-in-law and express your gratitude for your relationship. Or maybe you send an email to a colleague and let them know how appreciative you are that they're on the team. Or maybe you let your partner know how thankful you are that they're in your life. When you genuinely give thanks, your ventral pathway comes online. It can ignite a deep feeling of appreciation in the other person and pick you up out of a funky mood.

- Random acts of kindness: Small, unexpected gestures of kindness can turn someone's day around. They can be a sweet surprise, reminding you that there is good in the world. Research supports that random acts of kindness can be good for your well-being (Hui et al. 2020). The act can be big or small. Here are some examples of random acts of kindness:

  - Send flowers to someone.

  - Surprise your pet with a treat or toy.

  - Do something for your partner that they would appreciate.

  - Call a family member you haven't spoken with in a while.

  - Pay for the person's coffee who's in line behind you at the cafe.

  - Offer to help someone who's clearly got their hands full.

  - Let someone cut in front of you in line.

  - Leave a positive comment on someone's post on social media.

  - Write a thank you letter to your mail carrier.

We humans are like Wi-Fi routers, always in search of connection. Polyvagal theory helps us understand this on a deep level and clues us into ways to use our social nature to influence our moods and emotional states. Learning to use your social engagement system is a clever way to work with your neurobiology. While the social engagement system is shaped by past experiences, culture, and neurodivergence, one thing is universal, and that is that we all need connection.

Relationships can be like a double-edged sword, either being fuel for our happiness or fodder for our misery. But when we learn to use our social engagement system to navigate ups and downs, we learn to use the power of our nervous system for our own betterment, along with everyone else around us. Polyvagal theory speaks to the significant influence we have on each other. The wisdom is that to be a good citizen of planet Earth, taking care of yourself is a way to take care of everyone else, and taking care of everyone else is a way to take care of yourself.

Highlights and Takeaways

- Polyvagal theory emphasizes the innate human need to connect and coregulate with others, asserting that social bonds are a biological imperative for survival and well-being.

- The vagus nerve plays an important role in our social engagement system as it allows us to receive and send cues of safety.

- Safety is the foundation of healthy and meaningful relationships. Safety supports the longevity of relationships and allows us to thrive through connection.

- A lack of safety in our relationships can have significant consequences. Relationships can be the best or worst thing for us depending on how safe or unsafe they are.

- Because of our predisposition to form bonds, humans can coregulate each other. From soothing a crying infant to offering a hug to a grieving friend, coregulation is a type of superpower that we have because of our social engagement system.

- Your nervous system is contagious. Human beings are interconnected, and the state of our autonomic pathways can influence others around you.

- You can use your social engagement system to improve your emotional state. Whether that be through cultivating compassion for others or random acts of kindness, your social engagement system can serve as a coping strategy when you're feeling down and out.

Chapter 9

Homecoming

We've embarked on a remarkable journey together, my polyvagal companion. Kudos to you for your persistence throughout this transformative exploration of self-help and personal development. By now you should be armed with a wealth of knowledge, enabling you to understand both yourself and those around you more deeply, thanks to your newfound expertise in polyvagal theory. My hope is that I've endowed you with transformative insights, sparking daily revelations as you grow increasingly attuned to the nuances of your neurobiology.

Emotion regulation isn't the final destination; it's an ongoing journey. While some stretches of the journey may be smoother than others, leading an emotionally balanced life demands constant, intentional effort. Just as a home requires ongoing upkeep, so too does your nervous system necessitate regular attention.

With this newfound knowledge, you are now equipped to be the steward of your neurobiology. The responsibility for regulating your nervous system rests solely on your shoulders. There's no one coming to rescue you, regulate you, or take charge of your emotions. I know. What a bummer. While others may impact the state of your nervous system for better or worse, ultimately, it's you—and you alone—who holds the most influence over your mental, physical, and emotional well-being. This is both a blessing and a burden. On one hand, it's liberating to know that the power for mastering the art of self-regulation lies within you. You aren't doomed to wait for someone else to show up dressed in shining armor and riding some majestic horse. On the other hand, it can be daunting to accept responsibility. If you've spent a lifetime attributing your emotional state to your upbringing, focusing on barriers as excuses, or identifying as a victim, this shift in perspective can be startling. Yet, this stark reality highlights a critical truth: irrespective of external circumstances, the onus to manage your emotional state is yours alone.

No matter your past adversities, current situation, or future uncertainties, you are and forever will be resilient. Your nervous system is capable of evolving and transforming through even the most heartbreaking hardships. It has the power to learn, adapt, and grow. Therefore, resiliency is always an opportunity waiting to be seized. How you handled things in the past does not dictate how you will handle things in the future. No one is immune to stress, fear, or the various forms of suffering that are part of life. Yet embedded within your DNA is the power to get better at living and navigating emotional storms. You were built for this. This innate resilience, fortified by the knowledge of polyvagal theory, empowers you to harness your nervous system's remarkable capabilities. You are poised to embark on a journey of personal development, leveraging your natural adaptive capacity to master life's ups and downs.

Recognizing your resilience and that you can work with your emotions and stress responses grants you the freedom to view your nervous system, body, and mind as allies. This isn't to say that stress, tender emotions, and pain are enjoyable experiences; if that were the case, you wouldn't have picked up this book. Instead, learning to find your "home" suggests that no matter the external chaos, you always have an inner sanctuary to which you can retreat—a home that is intrinsically yours and that only you hold the key to.

"Home is where the heart is" is a saying I'm sure you've heard before. In essence, this statement rings true when it comes to our neurobiology and body. Home is where your nervous system is. This can be a liberating revelation for many. Though your nervous system will react as designed, responding to stimuli and stress, you now have the knowledge and tools to work with it rather than feeling worked by it. When you embrace your nervous system and learn to work with your vagus nerve, you take responsibility for your house. It is a sort of homecoming in which you come home to yourself. This final chapter is a way for you to come home to yourself, to your resiliency, your potential, and your biological potential to thrive.

Your Autonomic Critic

Who inhabits your inner home? I bet you have some welcome and unwelcome guests. Let's examine those visitors who have long over-stayed their welcome, your inner critics. Everyone has inner critics. Learning to understand the neurophysiological significance of your critics and how to use polyvagal theory to work with them is one way to create a bit more peace in your inner abode.

Most of us have some critical inner dialogue that consistently chal-lenges us. You know, the voice in your head that puts you down, calls you names, and tells you you're unworthy and unlovable. We've all got inner critics that we need to get right with. While that might not be news to you, here's something to chew on. Did you know that your inner critic is born out of your autonomic pathways? That voice was born out of states of sympathetic and dorsal overwhelm. Your inner critics are 100 percent a product of your autonomic stress responses.

Suppose you've been chronically stuck in sympathetic or dorsal activation because of an immense amount of stress or trauma. In that case, I bet you've developed inner critics who reflect those emotional states. And I bet those critics are more hindering than helpful. These are your *autonomic critics*, who are born from your defensive pathways. When you hear their mean words, it's information about the state of your autonomic pathways.

In chapter 7, we reviewed our autonomic narratives. The narratives that come alive in response to our autonomic pathways also give rise to some very critical parts of our psyche. Our perception of ourselves, others, and the world changes based on which autonomic pathway has the most energy. If your perception has been chronically colored by distress, you've probably developed inner critics that reflect all those challenging feelings you've been navigating. How could you not? Those critics are loud and can be very convincing. But they aren't accurate, and they pose the risk of skewing your perception and reality in an unhelpful way if you give them too much airtime. Your beliefs inform your perception, perception becomes your reality, and reality shapes your experience.

Perhaps you are someone who has been chronically hijacked by the sympathetic pathway. You have a history of living in constant states of anxiety, overwhelm, and fight-or-flight energy. In that case, you might have an autonomic critic who says you're too much, you're crazy, you're dramatic, people are judging you, or you're permanently damaged. That critic is born out of sympathetic overwhelm. After all, do those sound like the words of someone rooted in their ventral pathway? Not at all. Critics born out of our sympathetic pathway carry the messages of anxiety, hypervigilance, fear, and overwhelm.

On the other side of the spectrum, if you've been living in a chronic state of dorsal shutdown, freeze, or faint, you might have a critic who believes you are powerless, everything is hopeless, you are unlovable and unworthy, you're a shameful person, and you're doomed to be alone. Critics born out of dorsal shutdown carry the messages of helplessness, hopelessness, loneliness, apathy, and emptiness.

Does anything sound familiar here?

These critics pop up when the pathways that gave birth to them are activated. Their voices get louder the more dysregulated we become, and we believe them more and more based on how much or little connection we have to ventral. Therefore, the more skilled you get at hitting the vagal brake, the more toned your nervous system becomes. The better you get at noticing your internal state, the more likely it is that you will be able to shut those bullies down before they ruin your day.

Meet Your Inner Critics

Forewarning: This exercise can stir things up, like shaking a snow globe. I intentionally saved it for the last chapter so that you'd have the skills from the previous eight chapters to do it. It is inspired by Internal Family Systems Therapy, which is a therapy that helps us get to know the various "parts" of our psyche and personality. Internal Family Systems asserts that we are dynamic creatures with multiple parts that make up the whole. Everyone has wounded parts, critical parts, and even protective parts. We can use polyvagal theory to get to know our critical parts, which come to life in relation to our autonomic pathways.

With all of your newfound insights and self-awareness, it's time to get real and honest about your inner critics. This work might be a breeze for you. But sometimes, this exercise requires us to take a hard look in the mirror. The messages your critics have been feeding you may have shaped your relationships with yourself and others and define the way you're living. Taking time and being honest with yourself is the best way to benefit from this exercise. This exercise may take twenty minutes or more depending on how deep you dive into it.

Find a comfortable space free of distractions, and sit down with something to journal with.

Start by getting centered. Take a few cleansing breaths and become aware of your body right here, right now.

Set an intention to be honest with yourself so that you can grow. You will practice this exercise with self-compassion and a deep desire to transform into a better person. We're going to poke your inner critics a bit, so they might get loud and start kicking your nervous system around. Remember, this is an exploratory exercise, and if done honestly, it will allow you to gain more control over these critical bullies.

First, call to mind the qualities of your dorsal pathway. Allow yourself to reflect upon and even feel how that pathway feels. You might reference your autonomic blueprint from chapter 3. This pathway is where your dorsal critic lives.

Now answer the following questions:

My dorsal critic tells me that I am _____.

My dorsal critic believes that the world is _____.

My dorsal critic believes that other people are _____.

My dorsal critic looks like _____.

My dorsal critic's name is _____.

Before moving on to the next step, take a few moments to say hi to your dorsal critic. Even if you don't like them, try to observe them and acknowledge their existence.

Next, call to mind the qualities of your sympathetic pathway. Allow yourself to reflect on and even feel some of its qualities as your sympathetic critic starts to wake up. You may refer to your autonomic blueprint for quick reference.

Now answer the questions:

My sympathetic critic tells me that I am _____.

My sympathetic critic believes that the world is _____.

My sympathetic critic believes that other people are _____.

My sympathetic critic looks like _____.

My sympathetic critic's name is _____.

Again, pause for a few moments here and acknowledge your sympathetic critic. Say hi or simply observe them.

Your critics are always trying to help and protect you, even if at first glance, they seem far from kind and useful. Remember, those autonomic pathways are survival pathways. They are built to protect and defend you, and therefore, your inner critics are no different. Ask yourself, how might these critics be trying to protect and defend me?

What is your relationship with your inner critics like? How do you respond to them, experience them, and engage with them currently?

Are there ways that you feed your inner critics, fueling their power and strength?

How do you respond to your inner critics? What do you currently do when they get activated?

What's one thing you can do to change how you interact with them in the future?

Now, take a few moments to transition away from this exercise. Notice where you currently are within your autonomic blueprint. Based on what you notice, engage your skills from chapter 7 to turn up or down the volume. Increase your connection to your ventral pathway to shift away from your critics.

This exercise can take you to some deep places. If you have discovered that you believe what your critics tell you, that they're ruining your life, and that you'd have to make some big changes if you learned that they aren't true, you are not alone. Doing this kind of inner work is powerful for a reason. It not only offers personal insight, but it can also reveal how we might be contributing to our struggles.

Most of us unintentionally engage in behaviors that feed our critics. For example, if you have a critic who tells you that you aren't lovable and you believe it, you might isolate yourself from others. Isolation will then prevent you from experiencing meaningful connection with others. And that lack of connection with others then only leads to more isolation, which gives your critic evidence that it is 100 percent accurate. To change our inner critics, we need to be mindful of the ways in which we feed and empower them.

Becoming aware of and in touch with your inner critics is an ongoing process. You will benefit most from this work if you regularly check in with them and observe them with curiosity. They are always trying to be helpful, even if they don't feel helpful. The critic who tells you that you aren't good enough may be trying to defend you from disappointment. Or the critic who tells you that you don't deserve something might be trying to keep you small because you needed to act that way to survive your childhood. Notice when they show up, what you're doing when they show up, and try to meet them with kindness. They are nothing to fear. They are simply fragments of your neurophysiological experience and representations of your autonomic pathways.

Your Wisest Self

When you are feeling good, regulated, peaceful, safe, and happy, do you believe what those critics have to say? Or do you believe them a little less in ventral? Are those critics very loud when you're grooving in ventral vibes? Or do they go silent? Maybe you forget about them altogether. I'm going to bet that those critics zip it when you're regulated in ventral. So, guess what that means? The hurtful, scary stuff they whisper in your ear isn't true.

Your inner critics serve up lies and manipulation. They're based on feelings, not facts. If their accusations were true, you'd never question their validity, and their stories would remain undeniably true even when you were anchored in ventral. No one is unlovable, unworthy, broken, or too much. That's a fact.

Within you lies a reservoir of wisdom, knowledge, hope, and resilience. This is your *wisest self,* and it is born out of your ventral pathway. You can consider your wisest self to be your core personality. It is a compassionate self that embodies wisdom, calm, curiosity, and intuition. Within the ventral pathway, we each have an innate capacity for healing and transformation. This wisest self is distinct from your inner critics who harbor fears, traumas, or maladaptive behaviors. The wisest self acts as a confident and compassionate leader within you who is able to put your inner critics in line. The wisest self is strengthened by improving your ability to connect to your ventral pathway. More ventral = more wisdom and intuition.

Embracing your wisest self enables you to counter the overpowering voices of your inner critics. By developing a bond with this wise part, you pave the way toward becoming a more resilient, insightful, and wise individual, well equipped to navigate the intricacies of personal growth and self-acceptance.

Meet Your Wisest Self

This exercise gets you in touch with your wisest self and will help you counter those inner critics. The wisest self can be called upon to soothe an anxious, overwhelmed, or shutdown nervous system. Our wisest self provides us with a reliable home base to return to when we feel mixed up and overwhelmed. By connecting with this part of you, you can begin to quiet the inner critics and navigate life's challenges with grace and confidence.

This exercise takes around ten to twenty minutes, depending on how deep you want to go.

Find a comfortable place to sit where you will be free of distractions. Get a notebook and settle in.

Start by bringing your awareness to your body by noticing your breath.

Set the intention to be curious, open, and trusting in this process. Whatever happens is part of the journey of self-discovery

Bring to mind the qualities of your ventral pathway. You may reference your autonomic blueprint to bring this pathway to mind. Picture yourself feeling happy, peaceful, regulated, and safe. You're in your just-right zone—the best version of yourself that you can be. This is ventral at its finest, and you deserve it. This part of you knows things and has a keen intuition. They recognize that life is full of ups and downs, happiness and sorrow. They trust the process of life, know who they are, and hold out hope for the future.

With this part of you in mind, answer the following questions:

This part of me believes that I am _____.

This part of me believes that the world is _____.

This part of me believes that people are _____.

This part of me looks like _____.

This part of me is called _____.

Is there anything your wisest self has to share with you or anything you'd like to ask this part of you? You might turn inward to ask these questions and hear feedback, or you might actually dialogue in a notebook with this part of you. For example, you might write, "How do I navigate that situation with my mom? I'm at a loss," and see what your wisest self has to offer.

What does this part of you have to say about your inner critics?

Where do you feel this part of you in your body?

What can you do to strengthen your connection with this part of yourself?

Now that you've met your wisest self, make a promise to connect with this part more often. Remember, they're always with you because they are you. They are your key to resilience. And they're dying to be BFFs with you.

Write down any additional reflections you have, and when you're ready, shift your awareness back to your environment and surroundings.

This is your wisest self, my friend! Even if this was challenging to do, or you don't feel like you were able to snag onto a strong connection with this part of you, it's a place to start. If you've been BFFs with your inner critics for years, it might take a bit of work and dedication to develop a connection with your wisest self. After all, you two may have only just met and need some time to get to know each other. With time and regular connection with your wisest self, you will develop a stronger bond with this aspect of you, thereby enhancing your capacity to connect with your ventral pathway.

Here are some ways you can develop a stronger connection with your wisest self:

- Find an object or image that represents this part of you, and place it in a spot where you regularly see it. The visual reminder is a reminder to connect within.

- Take wisdom breaks throughout the day. Make time to center, turn inside, and connect with your wisest self.

- Journal with your wisest self. Write your wisest self a letter and allow your wisest self to write back.

- Talk to your wisest self. Yes, it's okay to talk to yourself! Whether out loud, in a notebook, or in your mind, ask your wisest self for guidance and insight when you need it.

Your Inner Sanctuary

In this chapter, we have focused on concepts that allow you to get to know your roommates who inhabit this inner home within your nervous system. Now, we'll shift to helping you construct your inner home, or as I like to call it, your *inner sanctuary*.

The inner sanctuary is an exercise designed to create an inner space of comfort. A kind of home base. Your inner sanctuary is highly personalized and a way to create an inner refuge of reprieve and retreat. Developing your inner sanctuary requires the support of your ventral pathway. Your inner sanctuary also becomes a means for you to connect with your ventral pathway. The sanctuary is a way to calm defensive pathways, quiet the mind, and find inner peace. It is a means for you to come home to yourself.

Creating an Inner Sanctuary

This is a visualization exercise. You can turn it into an artful practice through drawing, painting, collaging, or other forms of media that may speak to you. Depending on how you choose to engage with this exercise, this may take you fifteen minutes or more.

Find a quiet place to sit, free of distractions, where you can turn your attention inward.

Take a moment and center yourself. Bring your awareness to your breath, notice your body, and allow yourself to settle.

Now, call to mind all of the qualities of your ventral pathway, referring to your autonomic blueprint as needed. This is the pathway of wellness, balance, peace, and happiness. It's the just-right zone.

Think of your ventral pathway as your inner sanctuary. It was made just for you and is accessible only to you. This pathway provides you with the gifts of rest and restoration, very much like a sanctuary.

What image best represents your inner sanctuary? Get creative and use any imagery that speaks to you. Picture this in your mind, or get artsy.

Enhance the experience. Consider the following as you create this space:

What colors are present in your sanctuary?

What objects, animals, pets, plants, furniture, or pictures are in your sanctuary? Get elaborate and add anything that feels appealing.

What comfort items would be available to you in your inner sanctuary?

What do you smell in your sanctuary?

What sounds present here?

What is the temperature like?

Get creative as you envision this sanctuary. Add anything and every-thing that feels appealing, getting as elaborate and creative as you want. This place is for you and you only! Make it exactly how you'd like it to be.

After you've developed your sanctuary, set a timer for five minutes and allow yourself to hang out there. Soak it up! You deserve it.

Before you leave this space, remind yourself that you can return anytime. It is always available to you.

Next time you feel overwhelmed or dysregulated, you can return to this space by turning inward and calling it into your mind. Take a break here during the day to seek balance and comfort. The more you use this space, the easier it is to access.

Impermanence

An important lesson on the journey of self-regulation and transformation is that of impermanence. The fundamental truth is that everything is fleeting—from the weather to our emotions. In the blink of an eye, everything can change. Embracing the truth of impermanence can be a sobering reminder in difficult times, serving as a beacon of hope that everything changes, and hard moments are no exception. Life's only constant is change, and this applies as much to our autonomic states and moments of intense emotions as it does to every other aspect of our existence. The lesson is that no emotion is fixed or permanent. While sometimes it feels like anxiety or depression will never end, I guarantee you they will.

Buddhism and yoga philosophy emphasize that we inflict a whole lot of suffering on ourselves when we ignore the nature of impermanence. By exaggerating problems, succumbing to ego, or becoming overly attached to the present, we generate unnecessary pain. This attachment can manifest as a fixation on negative emotions, mistakenly believing they are permanent fixtures, or taking moments of joy and happiness for granted. When we believe that our current autonomic state (whether that's ventral, sympathetic, or dorsal) is the autonomic state we'll be in forever, we lose touch with reality. Nothing is forever. Not even the current state of your neurobiology.

The truth is that emotions, thoughts, and sensations are transient. They will come and go, rise and fall. Acknowledging the impermanence of all experiences helps us navigate emotional highs and lows with grace. When caught in moments of suffering, reminding ourselves that "this too shall pass" can be a powerful and sobering coping mechanism. Conversely, in moments of peace and joy, it's also just as important to recognize that "this too shall pass." This is a way to humble yourself and remember that your nervous system is always changing, evolving, adapting, and responding.

Reflecting on the law of impermanence teaches us the temporary nature of our feelings, autonomic states, and bodily sensations. Clinging to any emotion—be it distress or delight—only exacerbates hard times. Whether it's by labeling ourselves based on fleeting emotional states or chasing after a good feeling that has passed, attachment amplifies suffering. When we instead embrace the ebb and flow of life, we can experience each sorrow and joy with more presence and balance. The goal of healing and becoming more emotionally balanced isn't to never feel hard feelings again. Rather, the goal is to be able to be present and feel it all. The good and the bad. And to do that, you need a flexible vagus nerve and a resilient nervous system.

Riding Waves

When I think of the impermanence of feelings, sensations, and autonomic pathways, I can't help but think of ocean waves. Sometimes, those autonomic pathways feel like a tsunami. They're scary and overwhelming, and you're worried you'll come crashing down. Other times, you may feel the peaceful current of the ventral pathway, rocking you into a gentle, nurturing slumber.

Your autonomic nervous system ebbs and flows like the waves of the ocean. Sometimes, the seas are choppy, and sometimes, they're calm. But no matter what wave you are currently riding, it too shall pass.

As you think about riding waves of your autonomic nervous system, it can be useful to develop a mantra to lean on in challenging times. Focusing on this mantra when the seas get stormy will help you navigate the present moment and keep your focus on the fact that this, too, shall pass. The next exercise may only take you five to ten minutes.

Find a place to sit and reflect with a journal.

Reflect on the idea of impermanence, that everything is in constant flux and that nothing (most certainly not your emotional state) is permanent. No matter how pleasant or unpleasant, good or bad something is, it will change. No matter what, life moves on.

Now, identify two to three grounding statements or mantras that will help remind you of this fact when you're in need of a reality check. What are two to three statements that you can turn to in times of sympathetic overwhelm or dorsal shutdown to keep you grounded?

Below are a few of the statements I use. Feel free to use mine or use them for inspiration:

This, too, shall pass.

This is just a moment in time.

Ride the wave.

Once you've identified a few personal mantras, write them down somewhere you'll remember to look at them when the going gets tough. You might write them on your mirror, your fridge, your car dashboard, or the inside of a desk drawer you open daily. It's easy to forget about the impermanence of things when you're swept away in the moment. Place these sayings somewhere that they can serve as a lifeline right when you need it.

Time to Thrive

With so much newfound knowledge, it's time for you to thrive. What does it mean to thrive, you might ask? Thriving is the outcome of learning to deeply and intentionally care for your neurobiology. Thriving is an active process, not a passive one. When we care for our nervous system and keep our vagus nerve in tip-top shape, we are awarded a plethora of resources and opportunities to grow and transform into our best possible selves. That transformation comes from the inside out. Thriving is an inside job.

When you thrive, you are living your best life. You are the best version of yourself, no matter what terrible traumas and tragedies may come your way. Thriving is a testament to your level of resilience and how much you have learned to care for your nervous system.

Thriving requires the adoption of personal habits and techniques that collectively give you the fuel and resources you need to transform into the best version of yourself. Focusing on the adoption of habits that benefit your vagus nerve and neurobiology, you can transform your life, achieve your goals, and become the person you are yearning to be.

When we're chronically stuck in autonomic pathways of overwhelm and shutdown, and with minimal skills to regulate our neurobiology, we are essentially stuck in survival mode. Life feels messy in survival mode because you're living in protective sympathetic or dorsal states with little capacity to connect to the restorative pathway of ventral. Now that you've learned what your vagus nerve is, how it functions, and how to work with it, you can live with this tiny but mighty nerve at the forefront of your awareness. When you live your life with a constant focus on your nervous system, you will naturally start to engage in habits that are good for your neurobiology. The adoption of personal habits and strategies that allow your nervous system to be its best is what transforms you from a life that you are merely surviving to a life in which you are thriving.

Meet Your Future Self

In this final exercise, and my favorite exercise personally, you get to meet your future self. The purpose of this exercise is to set your sights on the goal. You read this whole book because you are in search of ways to better yourself. You're after something. You're after a version of yourself.

So often, we focus on problems. Our mind picks at the things that aren't going right, the ways you're letting yourself down, and on the problems of today and tomorrow. This is the negativity bias we reviewed in previous chapters. If you hyperfocus on problems, you feed your neuroception cues of danger and keep your autonomic nervous system stuck in survival mode. Where your mind goes, energy flows. Or perhaps the more polyvagal-informed way to say this would be, where attention goes, autonomic pathways follow.

Dreaming of the future I desire to create and focusing my mind on what steps I must take to get there has profoundly impacted me. What if instead of focusing on everything wrong, you put all that energy into dreaming up your best possible future?

Here's the thing. I bet that your desired future is full of good stuff. I doubt you would say, "Well, Rebecca, in the future, I hope to be struggling with panic, soul-crushing amounts of worry, constant drama in my relationships, and face down in the gutter." No. You would talk about your dreams, your hopes, and your vision. And I bet if you gave yourself permission to really dream that future, it would be irresistible.

When we allow ourselves to dream our best possible future, we spark awe, wonder, and desire made possible in part by the ventral pathway. Dreaming your future isn't just some hippy-dippy meditation. It is a way to ignite your autonomic pathways to help drive you to the realization of those goals. The feelings that can come from this work are worth chasing after. And they feel way more appealing than chasing after problems.

Get comfortable in a space free of distractions. Grab something to write with and jot down your reflections.

Take a few breaths to get centered. Slow your breathing down and release any tension you might be holding in your body.

Imagine it is some time in the future. You have taken the knowledge of this book and applied it to your life, and you are thriving. You've developed skills to engage your vagal brake, you can change the volume inside like a pro, and you're uber aware of your autonomic blueprint. Your nervous system is toned like a six-pack of abs, and you are neurophysiologically fit! You are living your best life, full of confidence, joy, and happiness. Stress happens because it's life! But in the future, you can navigate your way through those hard times like a pro.

What is your future self doing that makes this dream possible? What skills do they regularly use and engage with? How are they taking care of their nervous system? Write your answers down and get as specific as possible. It can be anything from "They practice breathing techniques every day, they set boundaries with people who aren't good for them, and they are always tracking their autonomic blueprint." Whatever it is that they might be doing, write it down.

What is this future self not doing that you are doing today? What did they have to stop doing to achieve this outcome?

What feelings and sensations do you notice in your body as you picture this future you? Notice and name them, and write them down.

Do you have anything you want to ask your future self? Or is there anything that your future self wants to tell you?

What are three things you can start doing now that will get you closer to this future version of yourself?

Write down any final reflections, and transition your awareness back to your surroundings.

When you focus on possibilities rather than problems, you motivate your nervous system to help you get there. Remember, you are resilient, adaptive, and have neuroplasticity on your side! The more enticing and desirable that future version of you is, the more motivation you will have to go after them.

Make it a weekly to daily practice to return to the vision of your future self that you started manifesting right here. It is a way to keep your eye on the prize and your nervous system motivated. Create a vision board, get artsy, cut out pictures from magazines, or do whatever it takes to keep your eye on the goal. I have personally found this strategy to be a game changer, and I use it daily. Every time I connect to my future self, I feel a warm surge of ventral energy and notice a sense of excitement and wonder as I envision all of the potential.

Your future self is waiting for you. Don't stand them up!

How to Tame Your Dragon

As we come to the end of our journey, I hope you are wrapping up this book better off than you began. If there is anything that you take away from this book, I hope it is the awareness that you can befriend your nervous system and better your life by doing so. Living is hard. Life is full of pain, loss, disease, and grief. There will undoubtedly be heartache and hard times, and your nervous system will respond to that accordingly. But we have a whole part of our nervous system (the ventral pathway) that also allows us to experience peace, joy, love, connection, and safety. Our nervous system was designed to experience the joys and sorrows of life. You were built for this.

You are a resilient being with a nervous system that wants the best for you. It is wired to protect and defend you at all costs. But you have to take the reins and work with your system if you want that life you just dreamed up. That life doesn't happen due to luck. Neither will it happen if you engage in things that actively hinder your nervous system. That life is possible if you choose to grow, adapt, and transform. And that transformation happens within your nervous system.

As I think of the relationship that we must create between our intellectual mind and our automatic or autonomic nervous system, I think of a dragon rider. Metaphorically speaking, we are all dragon riders. But most of us don't know this. Your dragon is your autonomic nervous system, which can be fierce, unruly, and very scary if left untrained. It, too, can behave in ferocious, dangerous, and reactive ways. And most of us don't put any thought or time into training it. As a result, your metaphorical dragon (aka your autonomic nervous system) can take you for a wild ride that can feel terrifying and out of control. That dragon will ruin your life if you don't train it.

Learning polyvagal theory is like an instruction manual for training your dragon. Your autonomic, automatic, nervous system of a dragon that is. Learning to work with your vagus nerve and autonomic pathways is akin to taking the reins of your nervous system and, in doing so, taking the reins of your life. While your nervous system can never be fully controlled, applying the principles of polyvagal theory teaches you what your nervous system needs so you can work with it. With patience, practice, and regular care, you can befriend and trust your dragon or your nervous system. And together, you make one heck of a resilient force to be reckoned with.

So be humble. Be brave. Grab those reins and ride into the sunset as the dragon rider you are capable of becoming. Ride on, Dragon Rider. Ride on.

Highlights and Takeaways

- In this chapter, we celebrate your journey through understanding polyvagal theory and its impact on self-help and personal development, teaching you to come home to yourself.

- Remember that only you can choose to improve your emotional state. You are in charge of your nervous system.

- Your inner critics are part of your internal world and are driven by autonomic pathways. You can use Internal Family Systems and polyvagal theory to change your relationship with these parts of you.

- Your wisest self is a useful resource to call upon to increase your connection to your ventral pathway.

- Creating an inner sanctuary is a way to use visualization to connect with your ventral pathway.

- Integrating polyvagal theory into your life is a way to transform from a state of surviving to one of thriving.

Acknowledgments

No one writes a book alone. I'm immensely grateful to the many individuals who have taught, coached, and influenced me along the way.

A heartfelt thank you to Stephen W. Porges for your years of groundbreaking research and thought leadership. Your work in the field of polyvagal theory has revolutionized the clinical conversation and profoundly impacted my personal and professional life. The depth of your insights has been instrumental in shaping my understanding and practice.

Deb Dana, your teaching and coaching have been invaluable. Your books have not just influenced me, but I feel your guidance in every clinical session. I'm deeply grateful for your mentorship and for making polyvagal theory accessible and practical.

A huge thanks to Arielle Schwartz. Your spirit, embodiment, and work are truly inspiring. You are a model for every professional in the clinical field.

To my beloved husband, your unwavering support and encouragement have been my rock. Your belief in me is not just a source of strength, but it's the world to me.

My yoga teacher training has been profoundly impactful in my personal and professional journey. My training is in Bhakti Vinyasa, and I am grateful to my teachers, Katrina Gustafson, Lisa Theis, and Michael Shankara.

Finally, borrowing a line from Snoop Dogg, "I want to thank me. I want to thank me for believing in me. I want to thank me for doing this hard work." So thank you, Rebecca, for not just writing a book to help others but for healing your wounds, for being brave in the face of challenges, and for the growth you've achieved following some very hard work. Go, girl.

I believe everyone should strive to make themselves proud rather than seek validation from others. Why? It's far more impactful to feel proud of yourself than to rely on others for confidence and acceptance. So, if you're reading this, take a moment and give yourself a pat on the back. Try saying, "I want to thank me for me." Life is tough, but here you are, pushing through and persevering.

References

Balban, M. Y., E. Neri, M. Kogon, L. Weed, B. Nouriani, B. Jo, G. Holl, J. M. Zeitzer, D. Spiegel, and A. D. Huberman. 2023. "Brief Structured Respiration Practices Enhance Mood and Reduce Physiological Arousal." *Cell Reports Medicine* 4(1).

Bandi Krishna, H., P. Pravati, G. K. Pal, J. Balachander, E. Jayasettiaseelon, Y. Sreekanth, M. G. Sridhar, and G. S. Gaur. 2014. "Effect of Yoga Therapy on Heart Rate, Blood Pressure and Cardiac Autonomic Function in Heart Failure." *Journal of Clinical and Diagnostic Research* 8(1): 14–16.

Cabrera, A., J. Kolacz, G. Pailhez, A. Bulbena, and S. W. Porges. 2018. "Assessing Body Awareness and Autonomic Reactivity: Factor Structure and Psychometric Properties of the Body Perception Questionnaire-Short Form (BPQ-SF)." *International Journal of Methods in Psychiatric Research* 27(2): e1596.

Carretero-Krug, A., N. Úbeda, C. Velasco, J. Medina-Font, T. T. Laguna, G. Varela-Moreiras, and A. Montero. 2021. "Hydration Status, Body Composition, and Anxiety Status in Aeronautical Military Personnel from Spain: A Cross-Sectional Study." *Military Medical Research* 8(1).

Dana, D. 2018. *The Polyvagal Theory in Therapy: Engaging the Rhythm of Regulation.* New York: W. W. Norton.

———. 2021. *Anchored: How to Befriend Your Nervous System Using Polyvagal Theory.* Boulder, CO: Sounds True.

Denson, T. F., J.R. Grisham, and M. L. Moulds. 2011. "Cognitive Reappraisal Increases Heart Rate Variability in Response to an Anger Provocation." *Motivation and Emotion* 35: 14–22.

Ferreira-Vorkapic, C., C. J. Borba-Pinheiro, M. Marchioro, and D. Santana. 2018. "The Impact of Yoga Nidra and Seated Meditation on the Mental Health of College Professors." *International Journal of Yoga* 11(3): 215.

Ganio, M. S., L. E. Armstrong, D. J. Casa, B. P. McDermott, E. C. Lee, L. M. Yamamoto, S. Marzano, et al. 2011. "Mild Dehydration Impairs Cognitive Performance and Mood of Men." *British Journal of Nutrition* 106(10): 1535–1543.

Gladwell, V. F., D. K. Brown, J. L. Barton, M. P. Tarvainen, P. Kuoppa, J. Pretty, and G. R. H. Sandercock. 2012. "The Effects of Views of Nature on Autonomic Control." *European Journal of Applied Physiology* 112: 3379–3386.

Goldstein, M. R., G. F. Lewis, R. I. Newman, J. Brown, G. Bobashev, L. A. Kilpatrick, E. Seppälä, D. Fishbein, and S. Meleth. 2016. "Improvements in Well-Being and Vagal Tone Following a Yogic Breathing-Based Life Skills Workshop in Young Adults: Two Open-Trial Pilot Studies." *International Journal of Yoga* 9(1): 20.

Hjorth, P., A. Løkke, N. Jørgensen, A. Jørgensen, M. Rasmussen, and M. Sikjaer. 2022. "Cold Water Swimming as an Add-On Treatment for Depression. A Feasibility Study." *European Psychiatry* 65(S1): S559–S560.

Hui, B. P. H., J. C. K. Ng, E. Berzagh, L. A. Cunningham-Amos, and A. Kogan. 2020. "Rewards of Kindness? A Meta-Analysis of the Link Between Prosociality and Well-Being." *Psychological Bulletin* 146(12): 1084–1116.

Innocenti, G. M. 2022. "Defining Neuroplasticity." *Handbook of Clinical Neurology* 184: 3–18.

Kase, R. 2023. *Polyvagal Informed EMDR: A Neuro-Informed Approach to Healing.* New York: W. W. Norton.

Kelly, J. S., and E. Bird. 2022. "Improved Mood Following a Single Immersion in Cold Water." *Lifestyle Medicine* 3(1): e53.

Kempton, M. J., U. Ettinger, R. Foster, S. C. Williams, G. A. Calvert, A. Hampshire, F. O. Zelaya, et al. 2011. "Dehydration Affects Brain Structure and Function in Healthy Adolescents." *Human Brain Mapping* 32(1): 71–79.

Laborde, S., M. S. Allen, N. Gohring, and F. Dosseville. 2016. "The Effect of Slow-Paced Breathing on Stress Management in Adolescents with Intellectual Disability." *Journal of Intellectual Disability Research* 61(6): 560–567.

Laborde, S., E. Mosley, and A. Mertgen. 2018. "A Unifying Conceptual Framework of Factors Associated to Cardiac Vagal Control." *Heliyon* 4(12): e01002.

Laborde, S., M. Allen, U. Borges, F. Dosseville, T. Hosang, M. Iskra, E. Mosley, et al. 2022. "Effects of Voluntary Slow Breathing on Heart Rate and Heart Rate Variability: A Systematic Review and a Meta-Analysis." *Neuroscience and Biobehavioral Reviews* 138: 104711.

Lee, J., Y. Tsunetsugu, N. Takayama, B. Park, Q. Li, C. Song, M. Komatsu, et al. 2014. "Influence of Forest Therapy on Cardiovascular Relaxation in Young Adults." *Evidence-Based Complementary and Alternative Medicine* 2014: 1–7.

Linares Gutierrez, D., S. Kübel, A. Giersch, S. Schmidt, K. Meissner, and M. Wittmann. 2019. "Meditation-Induced States, Vagal Tone, and Breathing Activity Are Related to Changes in Auditory Temporal Integration." *Behavioral Sciences* 9(5): 51.

Magnon, V., F. Dutheil, and G. T. Vallet. 2021. "Benefits from One Session of Deep and Slow Breathing on Vagal Tone and Anxiety in Young and Older Adults." *Scientific Reports* 11(1): 1–10.

Markil, N., M. Whitehurst, P. L. Jacobs, and R. F. Zoeller. 2012. "Yoga Nidra Relaxation Increases Heart Rate Variability and Is Unaffected by a Prior Bout of Hatha Yoga." *The Journal of Alternative and Complementary Medicine* 18(10): 953–958.

Mather, M., and J. F. Thayer. 2018. "How Heart Rate Variability Affects Emotion Regulation Brain Networks." *Current Opinion in Behavioral Sciences* 19: 98–104.

Muscatelli, F., V. Matarazzo, and B. Chini. 2022. "Neonatal Oxytocin Gives the Tempo of Social and Feeding Behaviors." *Frontiers in Molecular Neuroscience* 15: 1071719.

Ohlmann, K. K., and M. O'Sullivan. 2009. "The Costs of Short Sleep." *AAOHN Journal* 57(9): 381–385.

Olshansky, B., F. Ricci, and A. Fedorowski. 2023. "Importance of Resting Heart Rate." *Trends in Cardiovascular Medicine* 33(8): 502–515.

Ortmeyer, H. K., and L. I. Katzel. 2020. "Effects of Proximity Between Companion Dogs and Their Caregivers on Heart Rate Variability Measures in Older Adults: A Pilot Study." *International Journal of Environmental Research and Public Health* 17(8): 2674.

Park, G., and J. F. Thayer. 2014. "From the Heart to the Mind: Cardiac Vagal Tone Modulates Top-Down and Bottom-Up Visual Perception and Attention to Emotional Stimuli." *Frontiers in Psychology* 5: 278.

Pinna, T., and D. J. Edwards. 2020. "A Systematic Review of Associations Between Interoception, Vagal Tone, and Emotional Regulation: Potential Applications for Mental Health, Wellbeing, Psychological Flexibility, and Chronic Conditions." *Frontiers in Psychology* 11: 1792.

Poli, A., A. Gemignani, F. Soldani, and M. Miccoli. 2021. "A Systematic Review of a Polyvagal Perspective on Embodied Contemplative Practices as Promoters of Cardiorespiratory Coupling and Traumatic Stress Recovery for PTSD and OCD: Research Methodologies and State of the Art." *International Journal of Environmental Research and Public Health* 18(22): 11778.

Porges, S. W. 2011. *The Polyvagal Theory: Neurophysiological Foundations of Emotions Attachment Communication.* New York: W. W. Norton.

——. 2017. *The Pocket Guide to the Polyvagal Theory: The Transformative Power of Feeling Safe.* New York: W. W. Norton.

——. 2021. *Polyvagal Safety: Attachment, Communication, and Self-Regulation.* New York: W. W. Norton.

Rajagopalan, A., A. Krishna, and J. K. Mukkadan. 2022. "Effect of Om Chanting and Yoga Nidra on Depression Anxiety Stress, Sleep Quality and Autonomic Functions of Hypertensive Subjects–A Randomized Controlled Trial." *Journal of Basic and Clinical Physiology and Pharmacology* 34(1): 69–75.

Rosenberg, S. 2017. *Accessing the Healing Power of the Vagus Nerve: Self-Help Exercises for Anxiety, Depression, Trauma, and Autism.* Berkeley, CA: North Atlantic Books.

Shevchuk, N. A. 2008. "Adapted Cold Shower as a Potential Treatment for Depression." *Medical Hypotheses* 70(5): 995–1001.

Spangler, D. P., and J. J. McGinley. 2020. "Vagal Flexibility Mediates the Association Between Resting Vagal Activity and Cognitive Performance Stability Across Varying Socioemotional Demands." *Frontiers in Psychology* 11: 2093.

Stanley, J., J. M. Peake, and M. Buchheit. 2013. "Cardiac Parasympathetic Reactivation Following Exercise: Implications for Training Prescription." *Sports Medicine* 43(12): 1259–1277.

Vaish, A., T. Grossmann, and A. Woodward. 2008. "Not All Emotions Are Created Equal: The Negativity Bias in Social-Emotional Development." *Psychological Bulletin* 134(3): 383–403.

Wells, N. M., and G. W. Evans. 2003. "Nearby Nature: A Buffer of Life Stress Among Rural Children." *Environment and Behavior* 35(3): 311–330.